WHAT a RIDE!

FROM BOARDWALK TO BOARDROOM

◆――◇――◆

A Hustler's Insights into Business and Life

ROBERT "BOB" McKEE *with* JOHN NIKAS

FROM BOARDWALK TO BOARDROOM

A Hustler's Insights into Business and Life

ROBERT "BOB" McKEE *with* JOHN NIKAS

Published 2023

ISBN: 978-1-954342-06-4

All reasonable steps have been taken to locate the appropriate copyright holders of photographic and other material. The publishers apologize for any errors or omissions. Certain words, names of models and designations that are mentioned in the text are the property of the rights holders of the marque in question. Such words, model names and designations are used for identification purposes only.

Logos and trademarks are reproduced for illustration purposes only.

All rights reserved. Apart from any fair dealing for the purpose of private study, research, criticism or review, as permitted under the terms of the Copyright, Design and Patents Act of 1988, no part of this book may be reproduced or transmitted in any form or by any means, electronic, electrical, chemical, mechanical, optical including photocopying, recording or by any other means placed in any information storage or retrieval system, without prior permission of the publisher.

Printed and Published by

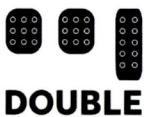

Double Clutch Press Essex Junction, Vermont

info@doubleclutchpress.com
www.doubleclutchpress.com

www.bobmckeeonline.com

FOR ENHANCED CONTENT AND ADDITIONAL PHOTOGRAPHS, PLEASE VISIT OUR WEBSITE

Design & layout: Jodi Ellis Graphics

Table of Contents

4	Foreword by Barry Meguiar
6	Introduction
10	ONE: This is Growing Up
30	TWO: Master Class
48	THREE: Adult Education
64	FOUR: Living the Dream
86	FIVE: A Whole New World
106	SIX: Reaching for the Stars
124	SEVEN: Calculated Risk
152	Epilogue
162	Acknowledgements
164	About

Foreword

The title 'What a Ride' is a great description of the adventure that awaits every reader of this highly entertaining book. Every page captivates your attention as you relive Bob McKee's life, from one exciting experience to the next.

In spite of all the forces against him and all his struggles and disappointments, Bob was not to be denied. His insatiable thirst for learning and succeeding lifted his joy for living, even in the midst of 18-hour days of non-stop hard work. A mere mortal would have given up long before he had a hint of success. And when that hint came, he was all-in more than ever.

A natural born salesman to his inner core, Bob could sell anything to anybody. His sense of timing and wording and opportunity knocking is a force to be reckoned with. Add to all that, his work ethic that took him beyond his peers and set the pace for everyone working for him was without compromise.

If you want to be successful in life, you would be wise to read this book carefully and imitate Bob as much as possible. He set the standard for everyone around him!

And he can do that for you as well!

On a personal basis, I've seen Bob up close and personal in the good times and the bad… and he's always the same person. The roots of Christianity, that were sown into his life in the early days of his life, have been tested by fire and proven golden. I'm thankful to God for bringing Bob into my life, as we have been encouragers to each other in our times of need. Bob is what you call a 'true friend' and the real deal!

Even more than our friendship, I'm thankful that Bob took the time to capture his amazing life in a book, for all of us to enjoy and learn from.

Barry Meguiar
February 2023

Bob McKee and Barry Meguiar, dear friends, trusted colleagues and close confidantes. (Author's Collection)

Introduction

"One win! Your choice, no tickets, no coupons!"
"Everything you see is one win!"
"Win a teddy bear for your love affair!"
"A prize and a winner each and every time!"
"Break a balloon to win!"
"One in and you win!"
"Drop the clown!"

Repeated 60 to 70 times each hour, all day long and deep into the short summer nights, I barked out these words and others, hoping to entice the people who strolled along the boardwalk in Seaside Heights, New Jersey into stopping in front of the booth I was manning and give me their nickels, dimes and quarters to play a game of chance to win a small prize. Sometimes their reward was a stuffed animal, record album or some other trinket and later T-shirts emblazoned with a famous logo or a Cabbage Patch Kid doll worth considerable money and in high demand.

Whatever was at stake on the spin of the wheel, the goal was to keep them engaged to get them to keep playing the game, allowing all that spare change to grow into more significant amounts of cash. Whether at Seaside Heights or Atlantic City or the other boardwalks scattered up and down

TOP: The town council of Seaside Heights, New Jersey committed to building a boardwalk in 1916, although it took five years to complete the initial construction phase. With few existing tourist attractions located on the Barnegat Peninsula, the boardwalk soon became one of preeminent draws along the entire Jersey shore, retaining that status through the 1980s.

BOTTOM: In addition to traditional amusements like a Ferris wheel, carousel and other carnival-type rides, the boardwalk at Seaside Heights also offered visitors a number of dining and entertainment options, including numerous booths like those seen here featuring games of chance.

the shoreline of the Garden State, the name of the game was entertainment. Prizes, even the more valuable ones, were just one part of the equation. What people really wanted was to have fun and an essential part of their vacation or outing at the beach was taking part in all the attractions at the boardwalk and few were as enjoyable as bantering back and forth with the barkers at the various gaming booths that

INTRODUCTION

lined the boards. Most of the employees at these wooden structures were high school kids, college students or other young adults, who were attracted to the idea of spending their summer break working at the shore, meeting new people and passing their free time in a resort environment where everyone in sight was smiling and having fun. I should know since I spent my first summer following high school graduation on the boardwalk at Seaside Heights. Unlike most of the people I worked with over those three months, I returned and eventually got a booth of my own. Eventually, I owned several and built a successful business along the Jersey shore.

It might surprise most people that know me from owning and operating the successful Driver's Seat retail stores in South Florida, building Autogeek.com into a world-renowned brand and multi-million dollar operation or setting out again into developing the popular line of McKee's 37 detailing and car care products, but what I learned about business wasn't gleaned from textbooks or listening to lectures in college.

Instead, the foundation for all these successful businesses was laid back along the boardwalk on the Jersey shore, one built with literal nickels and dimes, where I could look each customer in the eye and establish a personal connection with them. This book will look back on that time and others, reviewing some of the lessons I learned about how to run a successful business and overcome the inevitable challenges and obstacles that everyone encounters in life.

Like everything else in life, no one finds success alone and I'll discuss how to build a team and recognize talent, nurture close relationships with those around you and understand that having fun is half the battle. As I embark on a whole new business venture dedicated to resurrecting the SpeedVision brand with some close friends, it seemed the time was ripe to reflect on past accomplishments and contemplate all the factors that made such success possible.

I hope you enjoy the book and find it helpful in finding your own business or personal success. It has been an amazing ride and I'm thrilled that you've decided to join me on this look back.

Bob McKee
Stuart, Florida
February 2023

Bob and a co-worker making some improvements to a booth on the boardwalk at Seaside Heights, New Jersey. (Author's Collection)

INTRODUCTION

ONE

⋄—⋄—⋄

This is Growing Up

BEGINNINGS

At the start of the 1950s, New York City was the most important city in America, if not the entire world. Although times were tough during the Great Depression, like everywhere else, there was no question that it was the place to be. Once the Second World War had ended, things soon returned to normal. Athletes and celebrities rubbed shoulders with the rich and famous at hot spots like the Stork Club, Copacabana and Toots Shor's restaurant, while the Dodgers, Giants and Yankees were the best teams in baseball.

In 1951, more than 8,161,000 residents called the Big Apple home, which included me among that number once the calendar had turned to September 7th. It was a much simpler time, much closer to *Leave it to Beaver* than *NYPD Blue*,

The familiar skyline of Manhattan during the early 1950s. With the booming economic conditions that flourished after the Second World War, New York City continued to grow, with one in twelve American citizens living in the immediate metropolitan area. (Charles W. Cushman Collection, Indiana University)

RIGHT: With each passing year, traffic in New York City continued to worsen, providing strong incentive for urban workers to use public transportation. (Todd Webb)

ABOVE: All four of the McKee brothers used nicknames for their entire lives. In this picture from 1952, Bob's father, called Doc, stands second from the right, beside siblings Marlin, Nappy and Shorty. (Author's Collection)

but some things would still look familiar to someone from the 21st century. Traffic was bad, even back then, since it took almost 42 minutes in a car to cross Manhattan, which is about the same time it took to walk that distance at a normal pace. Parking was expensive: a garage in Manhattan cost $20 to $30 per month and an hour in a lot cost one dollar for two hours.

My father (and namesake) was raised in a poor suburb of Harrisburg, Pennsylvania with nine siblings. Born in 1916, he was a teenager at the beginning of the Depression and the next several years for him and the family were difficult ones. Education was considered less important at the time than eating, so he followed his three brothers into the Army at 16, serving in a transportation company. Following the declaration of war after the attack on Pearl Harbor, he served overseas in Cuba, continuing his duties in transportation.

Born and raised in Manhattan, Doris, my mother, had

ONE: THIS IS GROWING UP

Bob and Doris McKee pictured at their wedding in 1946. (Author's Collection)

ONE: THIS IS GROWING UP

THIS PAGE: Typical street scenes in Lower Manhattan during the first decade following the end of the Second World War. Most families lived in apartments, with lots of kids everywhere, the first of the postwar 'Baby Boomers.' (Charles W. Cushman Collection, Indiana University)

a much better childhood than Dad had, although few lived in real comfort during that time. She and her parents lived in a small apartment, her father worked in the city and her mother ran the household. Mom and Dad got married after the war and found a Manhattan apartment in the same building that her parents and an older sister lived in. Rent was a considerable expense back then, with a one-bedroom apartment in midtown running around $100 per month, while a penthouse on Park Avenue cost almost $12,000 a year! Living in close proximity to other family members back then wasn't unusual, since it was nice to have loved ones so close to help out with child care and errands. Their first child was a daughter named Donna and three years later I came along.

With his military experience, Dad had found a great position with Western Electric as head of transportation, where he supervised their entire transportation network between the various offices, factories and warehouses located in places like Illinois, Indiana, Maryland, Missouri, Nebraska, New Jersey, North Carolina, Ohio, Oklahoma and Pennsylvania, while also making travel arrangements for executives and senior management. At the time, Western Electric, a wholly owned subsidiary of AT&T, was one of the largest electrical manufacturing companies in America, primarily supplying components and equipment for the Bell telephone network across the country.

Dad's job allowed him certain privileges, such as being able to take me on tours of airplanes and even into the cockpits, where I could sit in the pilot's seat and stare at all the instruments. He was the go-to guy for all of Western Electric's transportation-related issues and was often called upon to help out in emergencies, such as when a big snowstorm would hit Chicago, where there was a big plant, and he would spend all night on the telephone helping to smooth out all the inevitable transportation snafus.

Like other businessmen of the era, Dad liked his cocktails and would have a drink or two, unwinding from the stress of a long day at work. He worked hard, drank often and had a bit of a temper. He was strict, which was hard sometimes, but he was a good father and always available for us whenever we needed him. He had an unusual quirk, however, thinking sometimes that he didn't measure up well compared to others, which pushed him to work harder, making his success more obvious to those on the outside.

ABOVE (ALL): Founded in 1869, Western Electric served as the primary equipment manufacturer, supplier and purchasing agent for the Bell Telephone System through 1984. For most of that time it was a wholly owned subsidiary of American Telephone & Telegraph. (Alamy)

ONE: THIS IS GROWING UP

Despite the occasional challenges and struggles, my parents worked to provide a stable home for their children and instilled strong values in us. Although it was somewhat unusual at the time, Mom worked too, which made a big impression on me. With so few families owning a car, lots of workers had to commute from the outer boroughs and suburbs into the city on public transportation. The average New Yorker at the time spent two hours going to and from work each day, either on the bus, subway or train. She worked behind the counter at Penn Station, helping travelers, something she did until my younger sister Peggy was born in 1958.

TO THE SUBURBS

When I was about four or five, we moved to the suburbs in New Jersey. It was pretty neat because we went from living in an apartment in New York City to having a brand new house in the suburbs. All of our neighbors were just like us – they all had young kids and traveled to New York City for work.

The suburbs were filling with young families, most using benefits from the GI Bill, earned from having served during the war. Almost all of the airmen, sailors and soldiers who had fought in the war had grown up in the Depression and all wanted a better life for their families once peace had returned, giving their children (which were coming along in record numbers to form the first batch of Baby Boomers) a happier childhood than the ones they had lived through.

Most of the suburbs were built on old farms and orchards, adjacent to older towns sometimes, like the one we moved to. I lived in a town called Fords, New Jersey, off the Turnpike, which had been established a hundred years earlier, but the new section, where we were, was filled with homes that had just been built. We all went to one school initially, but eventually new schools were built and those kids living in the old part of town remained at the old school. Everything in the newer area had appeared in the last few years, with great roads and green parks, which made it a wonderful place to grow up.

With economic prosperity banishing memories of the tough times from the 1930s, a lot of families had a black and white television, but there were no remote controls. If you wanted to change the channel you had to get up off the couch and walk over to the set and turn the channel selector, unless you were dad and then you simply asked one of the kids to do it for you. At least there weren't a lot of channels back then, fewer than the fingers on both hands.

We always ate dinner as a family, with dinner ready when Dad came home from work. Afterwards, he would have a cocktail or beer (or two) and sit on the couch with Mom, while the kids, all three of us, found room on the floor and watched our favorite shows. Particularly on Sunday night, we would gather around and enjoy the same programs that everyone else in the country was watching at the same time

ABOVE: When it debuted in 1910, Penn Station covered eight acres with a coffered ceiling in the waiting room that stood almost 150 feet high. (New York Historical Society)

OPPOSITE BOTTOM: Proclaimed at the time that it opened "as the largest building in the world ever built at one time," the original Penn Station was the transportation focal point for commuters in the Tri-state area. The booths where Doris McKee dispensed valuable information to travelers were almost always busy. (Library of Congress)

starring famous names like Ed Sullivan, Andy Griffith and Jack Benny, not to mention all the westerns like *Gunsmoke, Wagon Train* and *Have Gun – Will Travel*. Comedies like *Dennis the Menace, The Many Loves of Dobie Gillis* and *Candid Camera* were favorites too, as were adventure shows like *77 Sunset Strip* and *Route 66*.

Life at this time was actually similar to how it was portrayed on *Ozzie & Harriet, My Three Sons* or *The Patty Duke Show*. As a kid, it was a great time to be alive and be around at a time when technology was being introduced faster than most families could afford to experience it. When color televisions came along, few could afford them, but I remember when one of our neighbors purchased a new color TV and for the first time the entire neighborhood watched the *Flintstones* in color!

Most families went from the Western Electric Model 500 black rotary dial telephone centrally located in the house to either the Trimline Phone that hung on a wall or the Princess Phone, which was streamlined to look more attractive on a nightstand next to a bed. Later in the 1960s, the 10-button

During the 1950s, dubbed "The Golden Age of Television," most viewers watched with their families, allowing for the shows of the time to become cultural touchstones. (Alamy)

ONE: THIS IS GROWING UP

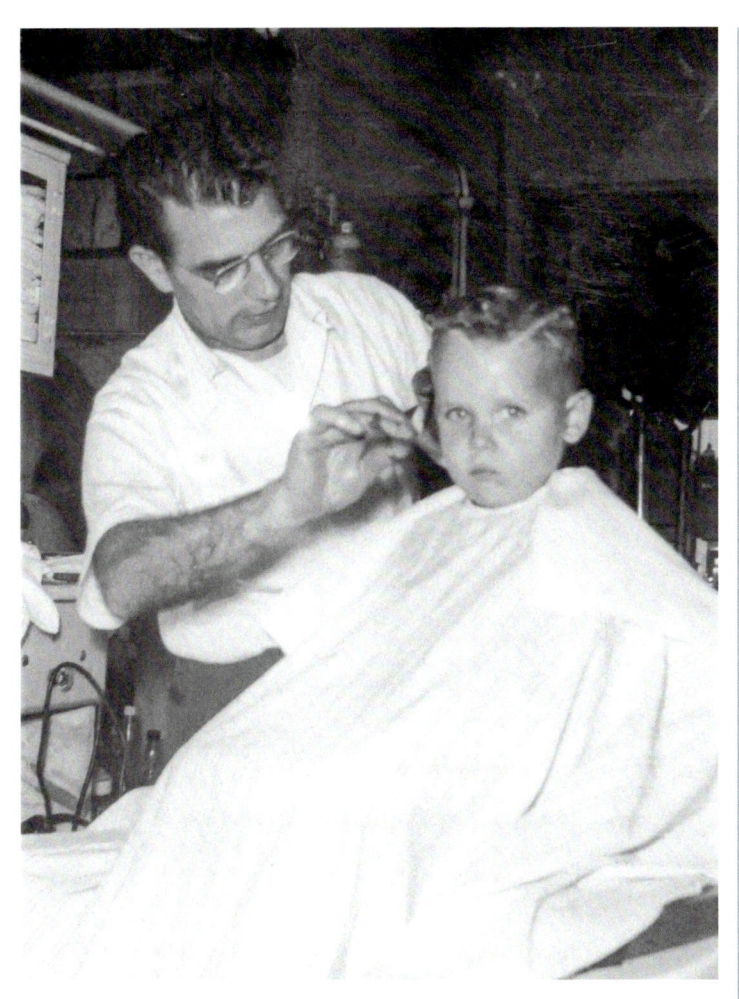

Bob receiving his first haircut from a local barber in New York City. His father and grandfather also patronized the same barber, making the monthly outings a family affair. (Author's Collection)

touch-tone or push-button keypad was introduced, and the rotary dial phones went the way of the dinosaurs. Back then everyone was on what was called a party line, which was four complete strangers sharing one telephone line. Copper wire was still in short supply after the war and several homes would be connected through a single loop, which could connect more than one line. Of course, the problem was there was no privacy at all since multiple people could be on the same line at the same time, each wanting to talk to someone.

Bob, Peggy and Donna with their mother at the house in Fords, New Jersey. (Author's Collection)

LEARNING PROCESS

Outside of life at home, the most important childhood influence was school, which was tough for me since I suffered from a learning disability called dyslexia, although it remained undiagnosed until almost four decades later. Unlike me, my sister Donna was bright, which made her a fabulous student who got straight A's all through school and later in college, but learning for me required a circuitous process that took a lot of time. When it came time to take a test, it always took me far longer than the allotted time, meaning that on most tests I would barely make it through half of the questions. When studying, my recall was poor and to understand something well required me to go over the subject matter over and over again. Reading was difficult and since the letters looked like a jumble most times, spelling a word like "Mississippi" was almost an impossible task.

I changed schools following the third grade and my new teacher suggested holding me back rather than starting at the next higher grade level. It must have been a blow to my parents, particularly with Donna doing so well, but repeating the school year did wonders since I had seen everything before and understood all the lessons much better. It felt good to be at the head of the class for the first time, which made me a more enthusiastic student. Unfortunately, the improvement didn't carry over to the following year, since I was starting from scratch all over again and there wasn't enough time for me to spend learning and relearning every subject.

Even though I was struggling, my parents never made it an issue, because their level of engagement with my education was never exceptional. They attended as many parent-teacher conferences as possible, but their focus was on earning a living and putting food on the table. In another time, like now, I would have been diagnosed with dyslexia as a small kid and then had a learning specialist help me overcome the problem with tried and true techniques. As it was, it was easier for me to do things with my hands, rather than learning from a book, which

An entrepreneur from childhood, Bob pictured with the first dollar he earned from doing household chores. (Author's Collection)

ONE: THIS IS GROWING UP

meant that a vocational education would likely have been much easier for me and resulted in more academic success.

Having watched Dad work so hard, and even Mom heading out to Penn Station every day until Peggy was born, instilled in me a strong work ethic. Actually, I really liked doing things outside, always mowing the lawn at the house in Fords and shoveling snow during the winter. When big snowstorms roared through, I would sell coffee for 10 cents a cup to the drivers who were stuck on the road that ran behind the house. It wasn't much and the quality of the coffee was about what you would expect for a dime, but it set me out on an entrepreneurial path.

Thankfully, I was pretty independent. For various reasons, neither parent was much involved with me during childhood, even though both were around all the time. Playing sports meant that most of the time I rode my bike to practices and games alone or with friends and when the whole family couldn't get to church on Sunday, I attended the services on my own. We were raised in a traditional Christian home and we attended one of the two churches in town, Our Redeemer Lutheran. The other was Our Lady of Peace, which catered to Ford's large Roman Catholic community, comprised for the most part of Irish and Italian families that had lived there before the war. Even then, spirituality was important to me, providing me with comfort at tough times and helping provide me guidance when making decisions in life.

RAISING THE STAKES

As middle school approached, I was starting to flounder and lacked direction since school was getting increasingly harder for me. I wanted to do something that I could succeed at with my time after school and provide some purpose to life. I decided that I wanted to deliver the late edition of the *Perth Amboy Evening News*, the local newspaper. Unlike most independent papers at the time, it provided objective political coverage and focused largely on news that affected the local area, ignoring most national and international events and eschewing gossip and chit-chat. Instead, what it provided was news about local activities in Perth Amboy and the surrounding area, which roads were getting paved, what sewers were being built and what was happening at the local police and fire departments. Published six times a week, except for Sundays, it was what people who lived in the area read to find out what was happening where they called home.

The first time I applied for a route, I was informed that none were available, which was disappointing given how eager I was to get a job. Realizing how important this was for me, Dad helped me write a letter to the circulation manager asking that since no existing routes were available, would the paper allow me to start a new one from scratch. Within a few days I got a positive response and the paper offered to provide me with 30 free papers for 60 days to start the route. Fortunately, several new apartment complexes were under construction and no one had laid claim to this potentially lucrative territory.

Unlike school, which was always a struggle, selling

A good athlete with excellent speed, Bob played third base for the Fords Red Sox. Nicknamed "Triple Mac" for his ability to take an extra base, he enjoyed playing various sports through childhood. (Author's Collection)

ONE: THIS IS GROWING UP

newspapers came naturally to me. I started off giving each new resident a free paper, never mentioning to anyone else what I was doing. Every afternoon, I rode my bicycle around the route I had laid out, seeding each house or apartment with a free paper and after two weeks started knocking on each door.

I would welcome them to the neighborhood, inform them I was the local representative for the *Perth Amboy Evening News* and said that I was starting this new route all on my own. I then told them how important I felt it was for them to get the one paper that would provide them with the news on what was going on in the wonderful new community which was now their home. Canvassing the new apartments and homes and sharing my story with the residents would have an even greater impact on me than just finding new customers for the paper. It taught me the importance of making a personal connection with potential customers and establishing a relationship with each and every one. Riding through my neighborhood on a bike gave me the chance to see the surrounding world up close, learning when a family moved in – or out – and having a real stake in their lives, no matter how small. I was helping them to discover what was happening in their communities, the things that impacted their lives on a daily basis.

Beyond the sense of purpose that the route provided me, I was also learning the value of money. When making collections, I would get 42 cents for the paper and most customers would give me two quarters, leaving eight cents for the tip, which was a big deal back then. A slice of pizza and a soda was around 25 cents, but a candy bar and comic book were a dime, making that 8 cent tip not look too bad.

Working a neighborhood paper route was a rite of passage in the postwar era, although modern critics would likely find the massive reliance on child labor problematic at best and abusive at worst. The practice rose to prominence during the Great Depression when children called "newsies" were stationed on street corners to hawk papers for a pittance. (Alamy)

Even more important, however, I was getting recognition for working that had never come my way in school. The paper had an Honor Carrier program, which recognized those paperboys (very few girls, if any, delivered newspapers back in the 1960s) who enrolled 30 new customers per year. Within the first two months of having the route, I was able to build a customer base of 40 regular customers, the only one in my district to do that.

With that important help from Dad in writing the letter to the circulation manager and not taking the initial "no" for an answer, I had built a very small, but thriving business. In fact, I was surprised to find out much later that I was in good company since individuals like Walt Disney, Warren Buffet, Bob Hope, Tom Cruise, Martin Luther King and even 'America's favorite car guy' Bruce Meyer, all worked a paper route when they were young. Even though I couldn't appreciate it at the time, it was the start of a successful business career as an entrepreneur.

CLEANING UP

I worked the paper route for several years, progressively building up the customer base and having fun with spending all that time outdoors, although the winter months were sometimes difficult. Eventually, it was time to move on to something bigger and I found a job at a car wash, working nights and weekends, in Menlo Park, the next town to the north of Fords. Home to Thomas Edison's workshop, it was there that he invented the phonograph and the first commercially viable incandescent light bulb. The car wash I worked for was a pioneer too, one of the first that featured a conveyor belt to transport the vehicle being washed through the wash tunnel.

Cars would wait in line, pull up to the entrance and then attach to the conveyor belt, which pulled them past all the washing and drying equipment. Despite the novelty of the conveyor belt, it was still a labor intensive operation, with two premium jobs: the guy that drove the car onto the belt and the one that drove it off at the end of the tunnel. What made these two positions so attractive? Simple! Those were the only individuals that got to interact directly with the customers, therefore the only ones in a position to receive tips. Even back then, it reinforced to me the value of customer interaction and how important those relationships were to running a successful business. What were the worst duties at the car wash? No question it was working in the wash bay, where two people, one on each side of the car, were equipped with a wash mitt and a brush. Each

The first automated car wash appeared in southern California soon before the Second World War, but it would take another decade to see them operating in widespread use in other states. (Alamy)

person was responsible for washing their side of the car as it traveled through the tunnel. With hands always wet, clothes often soaked through from all the spray and having all that soap built up on a person's exposed skin made it a tough proposition. After a shift, it wasn't unusual for those working in the tunnel to have to peel off all the layers of gunk that had built up over the course of an afternoon.

On Sundays, a special arrangement was in place for taking breaks. Rather than schedule each break individually, the car wash owner would shut down the entire line for 10 minutes. We would put down our equipment and each of us would get a cold soft drink and two hamburgers from the burger joint next door called Humphries. The owner would feed us burgers, which cost 19 cents each, and the soda that added a dime to the total. We would then sit down wherever we could find a spot and enjoy our meal, never appreciating how much things were changing around us.

During the first half of the 1960s, America was transforming into a different place than it had been during the previous decade. Business continued to boom, but more and more families were moving to the suburbs, seeking more space and safer streets and communities. Fast food restaurants and drive-ins were sprouting like wildflowers and outdoor shopping malls were appearing for the first time. Andy Griffith and Ozzie Nelson were still around to remind us of what was so great about the 1950s, but new shows appeared, more nuanced and less innocent. *The Beverley Hillbillies*, *The*

An ordinary day in Manhattan during the early 1950s. (Charles W. Cushman Collection, Indiana University)

ONE: THIS IS GROWING UP

OPPOSITE TOP: Peter Minuit Plaza in central Manhattan. (Charles W. Cushman Collection, Indiana University)

OPPOSITE BOTTOM: A typical automated car wash in the 1960s. (Motoring Images)

Dick Van Dyke Show, Bewitched, I Dream of Jeannie, Get Smart, Gomer Pyle, U.S.M.C., Green Acres, Gilligan's Island and *The Munsters* appeared, all getting laughs, while other shows like *The Avengers, Star Trek* and *The Twilight Zone* thrilled viewers and sometimes made them think. There was less time to watch television as I grew older, however, since work and school occupied so much time, not to mention that cars and girls were just around the corner.

Building on the skills I developed while interacting with customers on my paper route, it didn't take long to become the employee who greeted the customers and drove the cars onto the conveyor belt, which pleased me to no end since I didn't yet have a driver's license. Knowing the importance of tips, I really wanted the spot that had a chance to earn some serious cash, the guy that drove the car off the conveyor belt when customers saw their clean and shiny cars coming out of the tunnel for the first time. But going from the front of the tunnel to the back, like working one's way out of the wash bay, was a matter of paying your dues. Each time someone left the car wash, it marked an opportunity for upward mobility and an increase in earning potential. I began to see life as a ladder, and I was learning an important lesson – always keep reaching for the next rung.

ONE: THIS IS GROWING UP

TWO

Master Class

SHIFTING TIDES

I spent the final years of the 1960s as a student at Woodbridge High School, located in Woodbridge Township, the next town over to the northeast from Fords. It was a tumultuous era in America, one that left the innocence that had marked the previous decade in the rear view mirror. The assassination of President John F. Kennedy in late

For most suburban male teens, emulating James Dean's dress in *Rebel Without a Cause* allowed them to feel rebellious without having to act the part. (Alamy)

1963, when I was still in grade school, altered things for sure, but nothing that was visible to a kid living in suburban New Jersey. But over the next few years, there wasn't an American alive, no matter their age, who didn't recognize that Sam Cooke foretold the future when he sang that a change was going to come the year after the president was killed.

While President Johnson talked about a 'Great Society' and introduced Medicare and Medicaid, others were focused elsewhere. There was a war in Vietnam, a place that few had heard of before it started to appear in the evening news, protests over civil rights and a fight over integration that

American teenagers departing a middle school in the late 1960s. (Alamy)

affected the schools in the South, but didn't reach us in the northeast, where we had kids from all sorts of backgrounds. Our hair grew longer, our clothes got shabbier and we started to question things more than kids our age ever had.

I continued to work at the car wash through high school, which didn't leave me much free time, but I still attended all the school dances and football and basketball games that I could, which made for a pretty typical high school experience. I discovered both cars and girls, the former through magazines and seeing them on the street and the latter from having to sit next to them in class without having the kind of thoughts that could get you in trouble. Of the two, cars were more important to me at the time, especially since working at the car wash was exposing me to all types of different cars.

I figured since I had spent so much time behind the wheel of so many cars at work, it wouldn't be a big deal to start borrowing my parents' car, without their knowledge of course. Whenever the opportunity presented itself, my friends and I would pool our resources, which usually worked out to a dollar split among the four of us and take the car out for a spin. It wasn't much of a car, a 1961 Plymouth station wagon with a push button transmission, but it represented freedom.

TOP: As the 1960s progressed, civil disobedience increased to the point of violent protest. (Alamy)

BOTTOM: An advertisement for the 1961 Plymouth Suburban station wagon, which one automotive writer opined "most beholders agree... was hit with the ugly stick." (Motoring Images)

Taking care not to wake my parents from their slumber, I would push the car out of the garage and start the engine down the street. I would then unscrew the odometer, thank goodness they weren't digital back then, and we would drive around all night, taking great care to remember to fill the tank to the same level that it was when we had left.

All that fun came to an end when I got caught. Once, when I was 16, my parents went into New York City for the

TWO: MASTER CLASS

The least populated borough in New York City, Staten Island's proximity to Fords, New Jersey made it a tempting destination for teens out on an occasional joy ride.

day and I knew where they would park, since it was always outside an apartment complex that we all knew, and I had a spare key made without their knowledge. Well, I drove the car around for a few hours and remembered that it was a day designated as one to show support for the Vietnam War, when people would drive with their headlights on. When it's time to return the car, I get to the area around the apartment complex and find that the spot it was in before was no longer available. I panic and drive around some more hoping that the spot will come open but that doesn't happen. With no other option, I park it in the closest available space hoping that my parents won't notice when they return to the car.

Sure enough, they return and recognize that the something was amiss. When they got back and mentioned the incident, I tried to explain. I said that I just happened to be walking by in the same neighborhood when a delivery truck appeared right next to their car and needed to unload. Since I happened to have a key, which was impossible to explain in itself, I offered to move the car to allow the truck to take the space and parked it nearby, but had neglected to mention that to my parents immediately upon their return that night. My parents were many things, but gullible wasn't one of them and I was busted. Both of them flipped out, yelling and screaming, but I acted contrite, accepted responsibility and promised to never do something so stupid again.

For the most part, however, I managed to avoid serious trouble, but I remember once opening a letter addressed to my father, which set him off to a degree that I had never seen before. I don't know what was in that correspondence, but he almost shot me that day, teaching me a valuable lesson – never invade someone's privacy. We experimented a bit with alcohol back then, which wasn't hard to do since Dad was Irish and kept a lot of alcohol in the house. Before going out with friends, I'd skim an ounce or two from each bottle and put it in a single container and have a good time for the night, never realizing how much trouble I could have made for myself.

Back then, consequences meant getting caught and as long as the police or someone's parents never found out what we were doing, then it was a successful outing. Back when sneaking into bars wasn't too difficult, it wasn't hard to head into Staten Island and find a place that would serve us, notwithstanding we were still several years removed from the legal drinking age. As a father now, I understand

The Empire State building in 1965. (Charles W. Cushman Collection, Indiana University)

how reckless our actions often were, especially driving without a license and all the drinking. I tried to avoid trouble, but at the time, reckless pranks, joyriding, drinking and carousing all seemed like harmless fun, but watching my oldest daughter struggle with addiction for 12 years and experiencing all the horrors that go along with that terrible affliction, I understand how different things could have turned out.

GETTING CREATIVE

Having a steady income, no matter how modest my earnings from the car wash might have been, mattered a great deal to me. I liked being able to afford things. If I wanted a jacket and my parents did not want to get it for me, I could go out and purchase it myself. Even though I wasn't the best student, I hung around kids who were motivated, whether that was academically, athletically or working at good jobs outside of school.

A class that interested me was one of the few vocational courses that the school offered – a course in graphic arts. It included lessons in photography, film development and various creative design projects. I had a really great teacher for the course who was far more laid back than the other instructors and though it would be shocking now, since he was a smoker, he allowed those of us that did, to smoke in the darkroom, which made us seem like the rebellious teenagers we envisioned ourselves as. It was an ideal spot, since there was a lock on the door to prevent it opening it when someone was developing film and there was a fan and vent installed to discharge the fumes from the chemicals we used.

I really enjoyed taking pictures and I covered sports and activities for the school paper, which was thrilling when a new edition was published and included pictures that I had taken. Attending the school plays from backstage was a special experience and the feedback from the people in the pictures provided me with a sense of belonging that was lacking most of the time since I never considered myself part of the school's academic community.

When I wasn't in school or work, I would occasionally head out to the beach or a local park, spending hours photographing whatever was around. Sometimes out of all the dozens of pictures taken when I was out and about, I would come across one that made me proud to have created something so artistic. I loved using black and white film, thinking that it was better suited for more creative images and developing the film myself in the darkroom gave me a real sense of accomplishment, but nothing like seeing something that I had shot appear in the school paper. Somehow seeing my work printed for others to see was different and it still is now.

TRAINING WHEELS

Whenever I could find an issue lying around, whether it was at a waiting room somewhere or during a rare visit to the library, I read *Road & Track, Hot Rod* and whatever other car magazines were available. All that time at the car wash driving different cars for a few yards, joyriding in the Plymouth and reading about them, had made me car crazy. I finally had a real driver's license, passing the written and practical test with ease, proving that all the surreptitious driving experience I had accrued had been valuable after all. What made me different from the other kids in school was that I had saved most of the money I had earned from the

Not until the Mazda Miata's arrival, Britain's MGB was the world's most popular sports car. This is Bob's MGB parked at a Stewart's Root Beer Stand on the Jersey shore. Known for its hot dogs and hamburgers, Stewart's locations were a frequent gathering spot for local adolescents. (Author's Collection)

TWO: MASTER CLASS

THIS PAGE: One of the seminal moments of the 1960s, the Woodstock Music and Art Fair attracted more than 400,000 fans to Max Yasgur's farm in Bethel, New York. (Alamy)

paper route, car wash and other odd jobs which allowed me to get a new car, something of a rarity for a high school kid at the time.

I could have afforded something more practical, certainly something with a better reputation for reliability, but what I wanted, and bought, was a brand new MGB roadster, painted bright orange with a black convertible top. At a time when most of the cars in the student parking lot were jalopies or hand-me-downs from parents or older siblings, the sight of a new British sports car made an impression – at least I hoped to think it did. The base price was around $2,800 and with sales tax and a few options it cost around $3,000. I put down $600 or $700 and financed the rest, teaching me even more lessons, like the importance of paying bills on time and ensuring that there was always enough money in the bank account to make sure the check cleared each month.

As a high school senior in the fall of 1969, it was impossible to ignore everything that was happening in America, even though much of what was taking place seemed so far removed from Fords. The summer of love and the Tet Offensive had happened the previous year, not to mention the killings of Martin Luther King Junior and Robert F. Kennedy. It seemed that the country was ripping apart at the seams and even though the civil unrest that was spreading across the nation and making headline news in the

TWO: MASTER CLASS

papers, like the riots in Chicago, Detroit and Los Angeles in 1968 had avoided the suburbs, the counterculture movement was very much around.

Through most of high school I wore a leather jacket, looking more like John Travolta's character in *Grease* than Ricky Nelson, who we would have called a 'collegiate' at our school, but by the start of my final year at Woodbridge I had become a hippie. The massive festival at the Woodstock farm in New York had taken place the month before the start of school in September and most of the kids at school looked like they had been there, wearing their hair long with clothing that could have come off the intersection at Haight and Ashbury in San Francisco. Politics became more important to us, though to be honest most weren't too aware that others were much more involved and vocal in their dissent against the status quo, although that changed the following semester when 13 student protesters were shot at Kent State University in Ohio at an anti-war event. Despite appearances, I was still rather conservative compared to most classmates, and remain so now, deciding that hard work was a better use of one's time and talent than other alternatives, particularly if that meant 'complaining' rather than 'doing.'

ALONG THE SHORE

That following semester, most of us seniors decided to 'play hooky' and spend a school day at the shore and though I couldn't know it at the time, that experience on the beach would forever change things, proving that sometimes 'screwing around' can pay serious dividends. In New Jersey, the boardwalks were an indispensable part of having fun at the shore. The world's first boardwalk was constructed in Atlantic City back in 1870, drawing visitors to the coast seeking entertainment, shopping, dining and a wonderful opportunity to have some fresh air alongside the Atlantic Ocean. The Garden State is home to more boardwalks than anywhere else in the United States and nearly every city and town along the Jersey shore built a boardwalk along their coast and most of them have various rides, amusements and other attractions, including Ferris wheels, carousels, bumper cars and spinning teacups to entertain people of all ages.

The closest boardwalk to Fords was located at Seaside Heights, which has been described as the "Classic American Boardwalk." Stretching for a full mile, the promenade located between two 300-foot long piers was home to all the same attractions as the more famous one in Atlantic City and countless family-owned businesses like arcades, bars and restaurants serving pizza, steak sandwiches

THIS PAGE: Visitors to the Jersey shore could experience the myriad entertainment offerings on the boardwalk or sunbathe on the sand. (Alamy)

TWO: MASTER CLASS

and Italian sausages that have been operating under the same ownership for generations. But the real draw for me were the dozens of booths that were scattered along the promenade, featuring games of chance, where someone, for a modest sum, could win something fun, a memento of their time at the beach.

Even though I had been to the boardwalk at Seaside Heights several times before that day when we all skipped school to spend some time at the shore, something was different. Laying on the beach, hearing the people working in the booths making their pitches to the people passing by, watching the girls walking along the sand in their bikinis, all had an impact that had never been made before. That night, as we hung out enjoying our last hours of freedom before having to return to school the next morning, I resolved to come back and spend as much time there as possible before I had to grow up and become an adult. Little did I know that the boardwalk would have a tremendous impact on that process and greatly influence the person that I would become.

Knowing that graduation was fast approaching, I returned to the boardwalk and applied for a position at one of the booths that sold candy. A man named Bob Whalen recognized that I had no trouble working with customers, didn't suffer from

The Thomas A. Mathis Bridge connecting Toms River with Seaside Park opened in 1950 and replaced a much older wooden version that had served as the sole connection between the mainland and shore. (Author's Collection)

TWO: MASTER CLASS

shyness and hired me. I started work immediately following graduation and found that I was a natural, embracing everything that went along with hawking candy at the shore and developing all the skills that were required to become a success working in a booth on the boardwalk.

Typically, most of the people who visited the shore were from New York and New Jersey. Predominantly blue-collar, these were cops, firemen, carpenters, plumbers and factory workers, who worked hard all year and took their two weeks of vacation during the summer and brought their families to the beach. It was the highlight of the year for them and they weren't happy when it was time to go home unless they spent the last dollar in their pockets. It was an interesting contrast to how things were in our family, when most outings with Mom and Dad and both sisters meant a trip to the American Legion, which might have been a lot of fun for our parents but less so for us kids. With so many veterans around from the Second World War and Korea, the American Legion was a hotbed of social activity. Growing up, we spent a lot of Friday nights at the post, eating pizza while the adults drank. Watching parades with the Legion Color Guard were a treat, but was a much different sort of fun than those who spent their holidays at the shore had.

Since it was too far to commute back and forth from Fords to Seaside Heights or so I convinced my family, I lived in a Volkswagen van that had replaced the MGB. There were bath houses built along the shore where I could shower and, given the time and the prevalence of hippies all over, it wasn't too unusual a way to live. Rather than selling the candy like one would at a store, it was offered as a prize in a game of chance. I would convince someone using strong and entertaining words of persuasion to put a nickel down, which bought them the chance to spin a wheel and whatever the wheel stopped on was what the person received. If they wanted something bigger or better or different, they could put down another nickel and have another spin of the wheel and take their chances of getting what they wanted.

It was so much fun that I started working double shifts whenever I could, putting me in the booth from 10 in the morning until late in the night, sometimes not knocking off until 2 or 3 am the following day. My work ethic attracted so much attention that I soon developed a reputation among the folks at the boardwalk as the guy that would work seven days a week, any hour of the day for however long that someone wanted me.

I loved what I was doing, so much so that even when I was working a double

Board of Education · Township of Woodbridge

State of New Jersey

Woodbridge Senior High School

This certifies that

Robert Darwin McKee

has satisfactorily completed the course of study prescribed by the Board of Education for this High School and is therefore awarded this

Diploma

Given at Woodbridge, New Jersey, this 15th day of June, 1970.

Charles S. Famula, President, Board of Education
J. C. Cadwalader, Secretary, Board of Education
R. [signature], Superintendent of Schools
Louis S. Gabriel, Principal

Bob's diploma from Woodbridge Senior High School. (Author's Collection)

shift, I would spend the one free hour that I had between them thinking about how to refine my pitch and honing the fine art of getting customers to spend money, but doing so in a way that gave them so much fun they were happy to do it and most times would return again and again to repeat the experience. The most attractive part of the whole thing for me was talking to different groups of potential customers every few minutes, ensuring that no two shifts were alike.

It was a real learning experience for me, since the key was finding the right phrase that would elicit a reaction and make them stop in front of the booth, so I could get them to part with some of their hard earned cash. It was imperative to build a crowd, hopefully one that was several people deep, stoking their enthusiasm the entire time, knowing that a raucous crowd always attracted even more potential customers. When I started, Bob Whalen, who everyone called "Uncle Bobby" provided me with some pitches that others had used with success and that I practiced over and over, but soon I developed my own phrases and getting a feel for the right tempo, one that got people reaching for their spare change, or better yet pulling out dollar bills that I knew I could get them to spend if I found the right words to shout out.

Like lots of things in life, timing was everything. If the crowds thinned out, one had to slow down the pace, hoping that people would stop to see what all the action was about and when the area in front of the booth was packed it was important to speed things up before people got frustrated with the wait and went somewhere else. It was always crucial, however, to keep the prizes flowing, showing people

THESE TWO PAGES: Youthful visitors to the Jersey shore in the late 1960s. (Alamy)

TWO: MASTER CLASS

that there was an actual reward for their time and money. For folks on vacation, having fun was paramount and one of the best lessons I learned was the importance of humor. While lacking the skills of a professional comic, I got to where I could make people laugh and every last detail was all about entertainment. If I made change from a dollar, I returned it with a flourish, something distinct that made them remember their time spent with me. Whatever you do in life, make sure it's memorable, you never know how valuable that first impression can be.

As the end to the summer drew near, several of the kids working at the other booths left to return to college, providing me the opportunity to do something different. I always admired the guys that worked the booths that offered

RIGHT: A booth on the boardwalk at Seaside Heights that Bob operated with partner Frankie "Pocketbooks" Sommerer offered LP record albums as prizes. Fitted with a loud stereo system, lights and an attractive sign that Bob designed, it was one of the more successful booths in the area. (Author's Collection)

OPPOSITE TOP: The most iconic boardwalk in the nation, the familiar sight of the promenade along the shore at Atlantic City, New Jersey. (Alamy)

OPPOSITE BOTTOM: The beach at Seaside Heights. (Author's Collection)

LP albums, 8-track and cassette tapes, thinking them much more valuable prizes than candy and ones that often attracted cute girls. I spent the last few weeks of that first summer after high school graduation working games of chance that offered records as the reward for spinning the wheel, and as the days grew shorter thought it's time to do something better suited for an actual adult. The truth is, working down at the boardwalk didn't seem like real work since I was having so much fun doing it. Even with all the double shifts, the long hours and working into the wee hours of the morning, it was something that I almost would have done for free. Almost.

TWO: MASTER CLASS

THREE

Adult Education

WORK EXPERIENCE

At the end of the summer of 1970, my father offered to pay my tuition to attend Middlesex County College in Edison, not far from where the car wash that I had worked at in high school was located. The enthusiasm that I had working at the boardwalk in Seaside Heights evaporated almost immediately once classes started and all the academic trouble that I had in high school repeated itself in college. None of the excitement I experienced at the shore made the transition to the classroom, making it even more difficult for me to focus and pay full attention to the coursework before me. I lasted around six weeks and gave up, withdrawing from school and deciding to get a real job.

Along with a friend named Randy Jewks, I applied for work at the Ford Assembly Plant in Edison, where the first examples of the Pinto were coming off the line as 1971 model year cars. With production ramping up for the Pinto, which would join the Mustang on the Edison assembly line, there were several open positions and I was offered one on the night shift. A union job that offered excellent wages and benefits, located just 20 minutes away from my parents' house, it seemed like the perfect opportunity.

There was little automation on the assembly line and almost every part required human involvement to position and fasten into place. The supervisors had the best jobs because their sole responsibility was to ensure that the 10 or 12 workers who comprised their team performed their work assignments in a safe manner, building automobiles with the highest quality and precision possible, but the real attraction

Soon after arriving to work in Seaside Heights in 1970, Bob's mother and father came to visit, an occasion marked in this photograph. (Author's Collection)

THREE: ADULT EDUCATION

THREE: ADULT EDUCATION

was that they didn't have to man a station on the line, able to float around and supervise their workers.

I installed brake lines on the rolling chassis on the rear axles just before the bodies were dropped onto the frame. The assembly line was set up to build two Pintos and one Mustang in series, alternating back and forth like that all shift long. We worked ten hours each night, six days a week and completed vehicles rolled off the line every minute to a minute and a half. With so little time available to complete the repetitive task assigned to me, it required constant attention to avoid getting crushed as the steel body was lowered onto the chassis. Armed with a fastener and a tool to tighten it with, someone fed me the brake line and I had to attach it to the rear axle. I was pretty good with my hands, but after the first two hours of working on my own, I was bleeding from both hands and had to use duct tape as bandages since there was no taking time off to get proper medical attention for the injuries.

That first lunch break I remember looking around and thinking that there was no way I could survive in that environment. The speed that the line advanced was insane and the pressure for workers to keep pace ate up the new employees and spit them out. Most of the new hires never made it through three full days and I was proud when that milestone passed and I was still around. Randy was having an even harder time and during our first few lunch breaks together, which of course were actually taking place in the middle of the night, we passed the time wondering how people spent 30 years doing the exact same thing over and over again.

Listening to my co-workers during breaks, all I heard was how these people, most of whom were the same

OPPOSITE TOP: A representative image of workers assembling a Ford Mustang. (Ford Archive)

OPPOSITE BOTTOM: Ford Pintos on the assembly line in Edison, New Jersey. (Alamy)

BELOW: An image of the Mustang II assembly line. (Ford Archive)

THREE: ADULT EDUCATION

One of the most successful new models that Ford launched in the postwar era, the Pinto's sales fell precipitously following concerns that the location and construction of the fuel tank made it prone to rupture and explode during a rear end collision. (Ford Archive)

age as my father, wanted to do something different with their lives. I might have wondered what made them persevere, but understood completely once I received my first paycheck. A typical auto worker at a plant staffed with members of the United Auto Workers made about $4 per hour at the time, which with all the fringe benefits that the union negotiated, was closer to $6 per hour.

I thought I had earned good money from my paper route, then believed I was living high on the hog at the car wash. I got even more than that working at the boardwalk and it was more fun than I ever could have imagined, but earning more than $300 before taxes every two weeks was almost inconceivable. Even better, after 40 hours we got time and a half which really made an impact on the bottom line. I soon knew why people gave their lives to the line – it paid well, very well, and required not much skill other than having to master a simple task that never changed from shift to shift.

Most new employees that made it through their first week were guaranteed a comfortable living and a stable job, although that changed over the ensuing decades. The real hurdle, however, was becoming a full member of the union, which occurred after a 90 day probationary period. Back then, the union determined who was kept and who was let go and a personality conflict with a supervisor was a virtual guarantee that you wouldn't make it into the union. That's what happened to Randy, who was fired just before the end of his probation. With our long hair, most of the older workers dismissed us as hippies and that seemed to rankle his supervisor, who decided to force him out by placing this small, skinny kid on one of the most physically demanding stations on the line.

The station that Randy was assigned to was located in the pits, literally, an area beneath the assembly line where he was required to pull down the shock absorbers to allow someone else to fasten them into position. Even with all of his body

The pit on an assembly line, similar to the one that Randy Jewks was banished to prior to his departure from Ford. (Ford Archive)

THREE: ADULT EDUCATION

weight on the shock, he didn't have enough strength to get it into position, which allowed his supervisor to get rid of him for being unable to complete his assigned duties.

Around the same time that Randy got the hook, I received a more attractive work assignment. Released temporarily from having to work on the line, I was sent out to the large lot behind the plant where the cars were readied for loading onto the trains that delivered them to a lot in Miami, since almost all of the Pintos that we built were destined for a rental program in South Florida. Much easier than fastening brake lines to rear axles, I checked and locked the motor mounts and verified that the contact points were properly gapped and the ignition timing was in order, which also allowed me to drive the cars to position them for final loading. It was the most fun that I had working at the plant, but like most things in life it was too good to last and after eight weeks I was sent back to the line.

HOME AGAIN

As the calendar turned from 1970 to 1971, I was surprised to find that I had adapted to my nocturnal life working on the assembly line at Ford. I'd work all night and leave the plant in the morning, noticing that the parking lots at all the

The Seaside Heights boardwalk as seen from the water's edge. Skilo was a game similar to Bingo that was a frequent sight at booths up and down the Jersey shore. (Author's Collection)

local bars were filled at seven in the morning with the cars from the employees working all the other shifts. But living at home allowed me to save all the money I was earning and it felt good to know that all the hard work was not in vain.

As winter turned to spring, I found that the call to return to the boardwalk was too strong to resist and after ten months of working on the line I returned to the shore where work was fun and I was doing something that I truly enjoyed. Beyond the solid income that working at Ford provided, it also influenced how I approached things later in life. It taught me that while earning a good income was important, it was crucial to like what I was doing and fastening brake lines and working on an assembly line was less fulfilling than other options that were open to me.

Working a booth on the boardwalk couldn't match what I had earned at Ford, but it gave me the chance to follow the entrepreneurial instincts that had led me to start that paper route I had as a kid. I was 20 years old and coming back to

One of Bob's booths along the boardwalk operated as "Darwin's Records and Tapes," honoring his middle name. (Author's Collection)

THREE: ADULT EDUCATION

Seaside Heights that second summer was like coming home. I liked the people I worked with and loved interacting with all the customers who stopped at the booth for a chance to win a prize.

I repeated the same schedule from the previous year, often working a double shift sandwiched around an hour or hour and a half break. The difference was that this time I was in charge of not just one stand, but two, with more responsibility than ever before. I was working my way up the food chain and I got to order the prizes and had to make sure there was enough inventory on hand to meet the demand. When the new shipment of record albums arrived at the start of each week, I would look over the stock, pick out what I wanted and help unload them from the delivery truck.

While Uncle Bobby was the boss since he owned the two booths I managed, he was also the mentor who taught me everything that I needed to know to succeed in the amusement business. He stressed to me how important it was to control costs, an important lesson for anyone running a business of their own, helping me to recognize a good deal when one presented itself. The records that we used as prizes were close-outs and were available from several distributors, so it was vital to know which ones had albums that were in demand and would be attractive to potential customers, not to mention were offered at a price that made sense for us to purchase.

The velour outfits offered at this booth could be customized with heat transfer logos of famous designers such as Gloria Vanderbilt, Jordache and Vidal Sassoon. (Author's Collection)

Even though we worked late nights, I would socialize with the workers from the other booths when we were done for the day, drinking at the local bars or sometimes on the beach, watching the waves wash up on the sand in the moonlight.

THREE: ADULT EDUCATION

BACK TO SCHOOL

At the end of that second summer, the Vietnam war continued to rage with no end in sight and I had to give serious thought to returning to college since having status as a full-time student was the best way to avoid having to fight in the war. I had heard through the local grapevine that there was a school in Florida called Miami Dade Junior College, now a four-year university, home to famous alumni like Sylvester Stallone, Mike Piazza, Bucky Dent and Victoria Principal. I decided to major in education and minor in psychology, the former primarily as a means to maintain my student status and the latter because human behavior interested me.

With no better options available, I applied and was accepted, forcing me to bid the boardwalk farewell for the second time in two years. As an out-of-state student, tuition was more expensive than it had been at Middlesex County College, but I had saved all that money from working at Ford and found a cheap apartment and drove my VW bus down to Miami to find out whether college life would treat me better the second time around.

Bob pictured with his mother and father in the early 1970s. (Author's Collection)

THREE: ADULT EDUCATION

ABOVE: A VW bus and Corvair parked along the Miami waterfront. (Alamy)

OPPOSITE TOP: Bob, third from left, with his roommates from Miami Dade College in 1971. (Author's Collection)

OPPOSITE BOTTOM: Bob, second from left, with his roommates in their three-bedroom apartment. All five slept on individual waterbed mattresses without frames. The coffee table is a large electrical spool liberated from the scrap heap for use as furniture. (Author's Collection)

Almost immediately I was struck with how diverse it was in southern Florida, with far more black students in class than I had ever seen before and a vibrant Hispanic community all around me. I knew that the academic coursework would be challenging and that there was no little irony in the fact that one of the world's worst students was learning to teach, but I was willing to give it my best shot. In one of the first classes I attended, the professor told the class that he didn't care whether we attended the lectures or not, all that mattered was whether we passed the midterm exam and the final.

Hearing that made such an impression on me that I resolved to come to school every day and work as hard as possible to make sure that I passed every test. Knowing that I had to do it somehow made me more energetic and gave me the impetus to overcome the dyslexia that had caused me so much trouble in the past. Even better was the chance to put what I was learning into action. As part of the curriculum, we were required to teach as a substitute at a high school in Miami or at the college preschool, earning credits for our

THREE: ADULT EDUCATION

work as student teachers. It didn't take long for me to decide that, given my small stature, working at a big-city high school wasn't in the cards for me, so I chose to teach at the preschool.

One of the most interesting things that happened during the time when I was teaching came after I had missed a day for one reason or another. When I returned, two of the children from my class approached me and said, "Mr. McKee, we really missed you yesterday." Up to that point, no one had ever told me that and the knowledge that I had left an impression on them, despite their youth, made me pay attention to the fact you never know how you might impact someone's life, either positively or negatively.

For someone whose last real academic success had come during my second tour through the third grade, it was shocking to find out that I wasn't just doing well at Miami Dade, but that I was getting almost all A's. With each new class I continued to excel, taking more time than the other students to process all the lessons, but learning them as well and applying them when working with students of my own.

Students enjoying the sun in the Quad at Miami Dade College. (Miami Dade College)

THREE: ADULT EDUCATION

Don Shula reveling in the aftermath of Super Bowl VII at the Los Angeles Memorial Coliseum, where the Miami Dolphins completed the 1972 season with 17 wins and no losses. (Alamy)

During the fall semester of my second year at college, Miami was an exciting place to be, since the Dolphins were notching wins in bunches en route to the first perfect season in the history of the National Football League. With one semester to go, I worked even harder, wanting to continue my own winning streak of consecutive 'A' grades and when I graduated in the spring with an Associate's Degree in Education and a minor in Psychology, it felt like winning the Super Bowl. Having suffered from dyslexia all my life, that time at Miami Dade taught me that hard work and perseverance can overcome almost anything, even making an academic success from a student that was always in the running for the "person least likely to succeed."

With college behind me, however, I lost my protection from the draft, but as luck would have it, I was in the first lottery following graduation and drew a number high enough that there was no chance of the board calling me to serve. Breathing a huge sigh of relief, I packed everything into the VW, headed north and set my sights on a new goal. During the previous summer break, I had returned

THREE: ADULT EDUCATION

Miami Dade Junior College

Miami   Florida

Has conferred on

Robert Darwin McKee

the degree

Associate in Arts

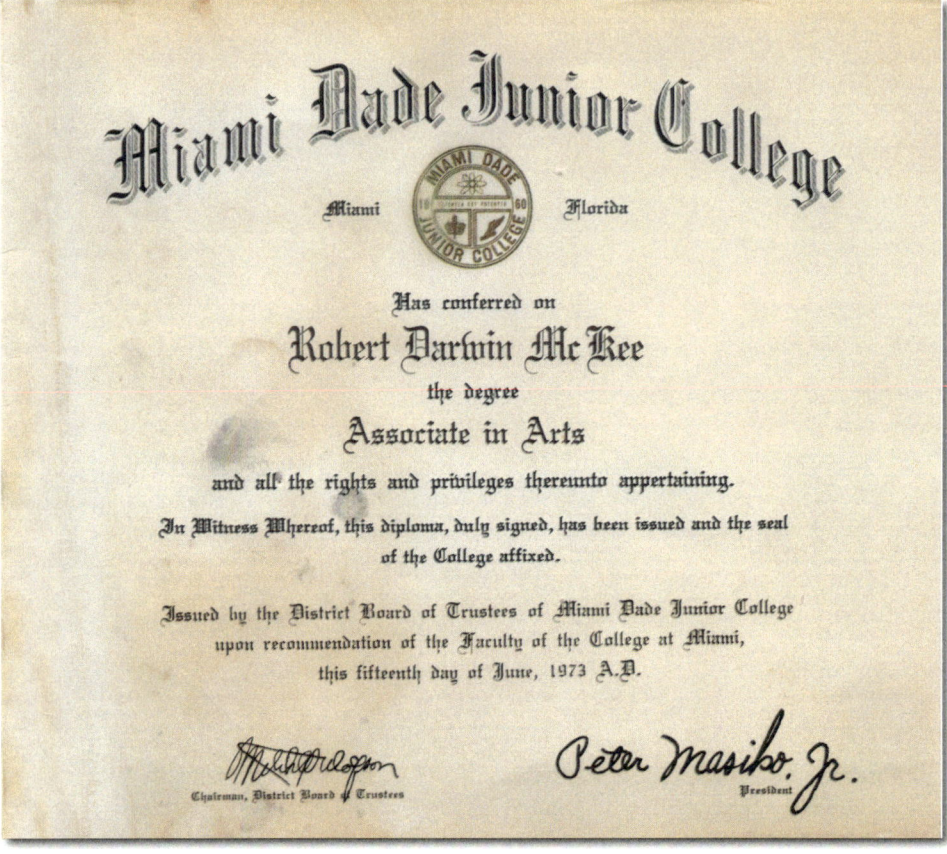

and all the rights and privileges thereunto appertaining.

In Witness Whereof, this diploma, duly signed, has been issued and the seal of the College affixed.

Issued by the District Board of Trustees of Miami Dade Junior College upon recommendation of the Faculty of the College at Miami, this fifteenth day of June, 1973 A.D.

Chairman, District Board of Trustees   *Peter Masiko, Jr., President*

Bob's diploma from Miami Dade Junior College.

to Seaside Heights, which cemented in me the desire to return as soon as I could to devote all my time and energy to becoming a concessionaire with a booth of my very own on the boardwalk.

ABOVE: Bob inherited this Pontiac Bonneville from his father. Originally painted in an anonymous tan, it was later repainted in this shade, which it wore during the time that Bob drove it. (Author's Collection)

LEFT: Looking somewhat forlorn, the boardwalk at Seaside Heights received far fewer visitors over the winter. The iconic Ferris wheel, located on the 500 block, was removed in 1978. (Author's Collection)

THREE: ADULT EDUCATION

FOUR

Living the Dream

ALL THE LUCK IN THE WORLD

Heading back to the Jersey Shore following graduation in 1973 meant a reunion with "Uncle Bobby" Whalen, who had mentored me since that first summer on the boards in 1970. He was the first to provide me with insight into the amusement business, allow me the chance to manage a booth and had given me the skills to succeed at doing so. Uncle Bobby was really a school teacher outside of the summer months, and like many other educators in the area, ran concession stands to supplement his teaching income. During the first couple of summers that I spent on the boardwalk, we would sit in a nightclub called The Chatterbox in the daytime (notwithstanding that I was well underage) and we would drink Miller High Life together and he would explain the hustle needed to make it on the boards, likely the first time in my life that someone treated me like an adult.

While his influence was significant and the instruction and advice that he provided was instrumental, his older brother Leo would provide me the chance to realize a dream – to operate my own concession stand on the boardwalk at Seaside Heights. Like his younger brother, Leo was also a teacher, one of four children raised in Lakehurst, New Jersey, the small town that was home to the naval air station

FAR LEFT: Lucky Leo Whalen. (Whalen Family)

LEFT: Lucky Leo's on the boardwalk at Seaside Heights. (Whalen Family)

FOUR: LIVING THE DREAM

where the German airship Hindenburg met its fiery demise in 1937, 11 years after his birth.

A long-time math and science teacher at Central Regional High School in Toms River like his brother Bob, his friends called him "Lucky Leo" in recognition of him avoiding combat after having been drafted late in the war. His lucky streak continued when he married his high school sweetheart after receiving his military discharge and during the spring of 1953, he happened to spot the Mayor of Seaside Heights, a man named Stanley Tunney, while attending a social function and inquired how one went about renting a space on the boardwalk. As Leo's luck would have it, Tunney owned several spaces and just had one become available, which had formerly housed a shooting gallery.

Leo leased that space from Tunney in the spring of 1953

Lucky Leo's in modern times. (Whalen Family)

FOUR: LIVING THE DREAM

One of Bob's booths operating under the Lucky Leo's name, which always helped in attracting customers. Leo's son Tommy had pioneered the use of plants as gifts, but the large tropical plants at this location proved too large for most customers to take home, limiting their prize appeal. The booth was soon replaced with one offering LP record albums. (Author's Collection)

with money for the initial payment coming from his savings and a small loan from the teacher's union. Since most of the concession stands were only open during the summer months, it was an attractive second job for educators, accounting for the presence of four other teachers and a principal during Leo's first year on the boards at Seaside Heights.

"I bought some used lumber from a building that was being torn down in Toms River that was almost 100 years old," Leo once revealed in an interview with a local paper. "I had to build the stand and the hardest part was nailing down the tar paper on the roof and then having to pour 35 gallons of gooey, sticky, black tar. After those three extremely hot days on the roof, my father and I had to throw out our shoes."

Leo's inaugural booth opened that summer and featured a wheel that customers would spin by hand for the chance to win dolls and stuffed animals. "It only cost a nickel for a space on the wheel or six spaces for a quarter," Leo recalled. His first summer operating the concession booth produced solid returns, so much so that he returned on the weekends after school had resumed, not closing for good until the end of October and reopening again the following spring.

FOUR: LIVING THE DREAM

Eventually, Leo assumed the leases for several other spaces that Tunney owned, later purchasing them outright, creating a small business empire in the process, not to mention helping his brother Bob do the same thing. Gifted with the ability to chit-chat with complete strangers about any topic under the sun, he was destined to work with customers. "It was always a friendly business," he remembered, "and it was always happy times when you met people on vacation."

There were good years and bad from a business perspective, but the latter were few and far between. Leo's first bout with hard times happened in 1956, when New Jersey state regulators ruled that the gaming booths at boardwalk locations throughout the state weren't mere amusements, but illegal gambling activity. All the businesses were shut down on the Fourth of July and remained closed for almost a month, when a sharp operator made a convincing

Two women on the beach at the Jersey shore. (Alamy)

FOUR: LIVING THE DREAM

case to the state that spinning a wheel made it a game based on chance rather than skill, something that wasn't gambling at all. The argument worked and the state relented, allowing the booths to reopen and there were no further issues, particularly after 1960 when voters in New Jersey passed a referendum officially sanctioning games with wheels.

The good years allowed Leo to expand his footprint on the Seaside boardwalk, which grew significantly in 1961, and continued to grow over the ensuing years, until he had the largest presence in town, including a massive arcade filled with pinball machines. The polar opposite from his brother, who was a hustler from the word go, Leo was more dignified, almost a statesman. He never drank, dressed well (unlike Uncle Bobby) and everything that he operated had an air of class about it.

When I returned after graduation, Leo offered to lease a concession stand space to me, rather than me having to operate one as an employee for his brother. He looked at me and said, "You want a shot, kid? I can make $10,000 from a stand and if you want to rent one, it'll cost $10,000, because you'll need to replace that income."

It was the chance that I had wanted and I seized it with both hands. With what savings were left after two years of tuition payments, I went about establishing the business of my dreams, where everything that I had learned could be tested in action, leaning on all the experience from the paper route, hustling for tips at the car wash, barking on the boardwalks for several summers and even working on the assembly line at Ford and studying psychology at school to make it happen. It was harder than I thought, but ultimately more rewarding than I ever could have imagined at the start.

STANDING OUT FROM THE CROWD

With so many similar booths on the boardwalk, it was understandable that there was considerable overlap in the prizes that each concessionaire offered, whether that was stuffed animals, posters, record albums or other items, which made it imperative to do something to make an impression with people. You had to know what the potential customers wanted and in the early days I focused primarily on music, getting LP albums and 8-track cassettes from the same distributors as when Uncle Bobby trusted me to do the ordering. But now that my money was at risk, the stakes were even higher, getting the right inventory at an attractive price could mean the difference between success or failure, which meant sourcing close-outs from the record stores and sometimes items of questionable background, though I never asked questions and rarely wanted to know where something had come from.

Controlling margins were crucial too, perhaps even more so. If a prize had cost me $5, it required me to earn $10 from customers to make it worthwhile. With four quarters to a dollar, that meant that I needed to have 40 spaces on

Bob at one of his booths in the 1980s. (Author's Collection)

FOUR: LIVING THE DREAM

One of Bob's booths offering painter's caps with band names silk screened on them as prizes. This image was taken late in the season, when the cost of spinning the wheel was reduced from a quarter to 10 cents, helping attract more price conscious locals. (Author's Collection)

the wheel, board or whatever other mechanism of chance was used, such that over time, the percentages worked out to make the right profit margin. If an item cost $10, then I needed something with 80 numbers to cover the increased cost of the prize. Occasionally, to make the game seem more attractive, I would reduce the number of spaces, sometimes to as few as four, but then require the customer to win six times, which made the odds the same as playing a game with more spaces.

The real question I had to answer, however, was how to attract customers and get them to stop, especially when there were 10 to 12 other booths with the same exact stuff? I came up with the idea to get good stereo equipment, not the old stuff that the other operators had to draw people in. You turn on the latest hot song and pump up the volume and suddenly everyone walking around is drawn to your spot like a moth to the flame, particularly since most of the customers that I catered to were like trolls, who mostly came out at night.

FOUR: LIVING THE DREAM

Terry cloth and velour sunsuits offered at one of Bob's booths. (Author's Collection)

Like in every other business, most competitive advantages are short-lived and the boards were no exception since everyone else soon decided to do the same thing, making it sound like a rock concert with all the music blaring. I then decided to put up some track lights, since there was a gap between the albums on the back wall where they were displayed. I rigged them to flash and that drew people in until everyone else on the boards followed my lead, evaporating the edge that I had worked so hard to create.

I realized that my ultimate success depended on being able to get people to spend money and that required either getting each customer to spend more or increasing the total number of customers. The next year I had a company cut channels in the booth that were straight and of uniform depth, allowing me to make the lights appear more professional. I then installed color bulbs into the strands and rigged it so that the strands flashed in time with the music and that was a huge advantage until others adopted the same innovation.

FOUR: LIVING THE DREAM

Sometimes we had to rely on old fashioned shilling and I would get staff to walk around with giant stuffed animals or other hot prizes so that potential customers would see them and ask what booth they had come from and at other times seed a crowd with shills to stoke its enthusiasm. With the pressure to cover the cost of the lease payments always present, I also decided to stretch out the season beyond the late spring and summer months, since even in the fall folks would drive down to the shore to take a drive and walk the boards. Another advantage to working additional days was that most of the concessionaires returned to their regular jobs at the end of the summer, which meant less competition since there were fewer booths open.

When the weather turned colder, I erected an awning in front of the booth and bought a space heater and some chairs that were placed on a plastic sheet on the wooden boards. It was great for business, since people would see the awning and the heater, sit down and take their jackets off, which

These hanging house plants were more portable and proved more popular than the tropical variety offered at an earlier booth. (Author's Collection)

Bob, far right, with Doreen and their friend Joe Bruno at Jack and Bill's, a local boardwalk watering hole that was popular with the concessionaires, who would meet there to discuss business and talk about new game ideas that could attract more customers. (Author's Collection)

made them want to express their gratitude by spinning the wheel. I was able to squeeze out an extra $10,000 to $15,000 a year just by working more than anyone else.

Over the rest of the decade, I increased the number of booths that I operated, eventually running six on the boardwalk at Seaside Heights and Seaside Park. Most of the primary leaseholders had at least that many and in some cases much more. Inevitably, some booths underperformed compared to others, which made it easier to approach their operators about sub-leasing these spaces, since it was easier for them to collect the rent and leave the headache of running them to someone else.

FOUR: LIVING THE DREAM

It was a competitive environment and not operating throughout the entire year increased the pressure to keep each booth running at optimum efficiency. If a booth wasn't pulling its weight at the start of June, I would replace the game or the prizes, sometimes both, until finding the right formula. When this happened, we would literally do all the work in a single night, which was really just a few hours since no one was allowed on the boardwalk from two to six in the morning.

LP record albums were a perennial favorite. Note the lights between the prize rows. (Author's Collection)

With more booths to run, we had to implement various games, beyond the standard spinning wheel of chance. We had one where the players shot a water gun into the mouth of a clown or monkey that would fill a balloon and the winner was the one that accomplished the task first. The more players that competed in a single game increased the size of the prize awarded. There was a booth with hundreds of balloons attached to the board at the back and a player would receive 3 to 5 darts to use to attempt to pierce a balloon, with everyone puncturing a balloon receiving something and multiple successes increasing the value of the prize, which we described as a "step-up" game that meant winning was easy, but getting something valuable required someone to step-up and keep playing to win the big prize.

One of the most entertaining booths on the entire boardwalk was called "Drop the Clown," a standard carnival dunk-booth that would reward someone hitting the target with the satisfying and always entertaining sight of an employee dressed as clown getting drenched after falling into a pool of water. We also featured other familiar games, like shooting basketballs into a hoop or attempting to get a softball into a wicker basket.

Whatever the game, there are certain business fundamentals that never change, whether you're running a Fortune 500 company or a booth on the boards along the Jersey shore. One of the most important is to hire good people, and while the kids that worked the boardwalk often lacked experience, it was vital for them to have good interpersonal skills and a solid work ethic.

It wasn't easy to interview someone and know that they possessed the talent to succeed, but those with good personalities had a leg up on the competition. We called

A family photo taken at Seaside Heights in the late 1970s. (Author's Collection)

FOUR: LIVING THE DREAM

LEFT: Bob flanked by sisters Peggy and Donna. (Author's Collection)

BOTTOM: The family posed beside Bob's Volkswagen Scirocco. The vehicle later wore a personalized license plate that read "ONE WIN."

FOUR: LIVING THE DREAM

THIS PAGE: Scenes from a typical day on the Jersey shore. (Alamy)

FOUR: LIVING THE DREAM

someone with real skills an agent, an individual with the moxie and the bantering ability to keep a game going, enticing the customer to keep putting down increasing amounts of cash for the chance to win the bigger prizes. That's where my minor in psychology paid off, understanding what motivated people to play and then coming up with a pitch that resonated with them. Interacting with people also made it easier to pass the time, studying each player and experimenting with different techniques to determine which ones were more successful.

Often, I relied on recommendations from others in making hiring decisions, who might tell me that they had a relative that was looking for work. As it transpired, most of the staff working for me were females, not for a particular reason but they did tend to work harder and complain less than their male counterparts. It was still important, even with low-paid employees to treat them well. Even though I offered the same wages as the other operators, if we were having a slow spell during the week, I would close down the booth(s) for a few hours in the middle of the day and rent jet-skis so that everyone could have some fun. No one else did that and I think it made the staff work harder, knowing that their boss cared about them.

SOUTH FOR THE WINTER

Having always learned from watching mentors like Uncle Bobby and Lucky Leo, I followed most of the concessionaires south for the winter. Most of them had second homes in Florida, where the teachers and other school employees would spend their Christmas breaks and the others would escape the cold of the Northeast until things warmed up again in the spring.

Whether a concessionaire had experienced a good or poor season on the boards never affected their decision to head to Florida in the winter and whatever money was with them upon their arrival was entirely spent whenever the time came to head back to work on the boardwalk. Thankfully, an entire economic ecosystem existed along the Jersey shore to cater to the boardwalk concessionaires.

In Seaside Heights, there was a local bank that extended credit to us, since most of us needed around $10,000 per booth to handle construction and renovation costs, purchase inventory and cover the initial expense of hiring staff. The bank would always provide us short term loans, provided that payment in full was made by the Fourth of July, which was the date when most of us had to start making our payments on our leases. The same situation existed at the local lumber yard, where we purchased supplies to construct new booths or renovate existing ones. It was a simpler time, an era when credit checks weren't required and a handshake was enough to seal a deal.

As someone who had spent their entire academic career in the back of the class, excepting the two years that I spent at Miami Dade Junior College, it felt good to know that someone was willing to take a financial risk on a punk kid like me. But all that money that was extended us increased the pressure commensurately and I spent countless hours devising new and innovative ways to keep people interested and spending their hard earned cash at the booths. I really enjoyed, however, sitting down with the other concessionaires and coming up with new games or talking about the next hot prize that would attract customers.

Sometimes, especially as I became a veteran, I would wait to see who had the good items and then find their supplier and offer to pay more to get priority for new inventory. One of the biggest successes that we had were Cabbage Patch kids. Even though the retail price for them was originally $21, the problem was that there was almost no inventory around, with whatever stock on hand selling out almost immediately. I would pay people to stand in line at stores to purchase them and then put them in a booth, knowing that people would fork over substantially more than I paid for the chance to win one.

Shoppers lined up to purchase Cabbage Patch Kid dolls in 1983. (Alamy)

Eventually, I found a supplier that could get me 20-foot shipping containers filled with them and we would price the games so that it might take one or two hundred dollars to take one home. Since we had a monopoly on them, I kept my source a secret, which paid off when I started supplying them to retailers in Florida at $125 per doll. Demand

FOUR: LIVING THE DREAM

was so high, that these stores could offer them for $250 and still sell each and every one that they could get their hands on. I never knew where my supplier got the dolls from, but I suspect that he had people all throughout the area camping out at every store to get them whenever a shipment would arrive, although being in New Jersey one could never rule out more sophisticated or nefarious methods. All I know is 1983 became a Cabbage Patch summer and we made a killing on them.

END OF AN ERA

It was fortuitous that the summer of 1983 was such a success, since conditions along the boardwalks had changed over the past five years. The shift had begun back in 1978, when Resorts International became the first casino to open in Atlantic City, taking advantage of a new law that had passed in New Jersey allowing for legalized gambling in the city. Initially, the casino, the first to open outside Nevada, was limited to operating for only 18 hours per day, although that

Gamblers waiting to enter the Resorts International Casino in Atlantic City. (NJ Press)

FOUR: LIVING THE DREAM

restriction would erode in subsequent years until gambling was allowed seven days a week, day and night. It didn't take long for other casinos to open and before long there were nine of them operating along the Atlantic City boardwalk and in the adjacent marina district.

Within a few years, competition from the casinos caused significant harm to the boardwalk businesses throughout the state. Limited to offering prizes at the time that were worth $25 or less, it was difficult to inspire excitement in customers when, for $10 they could take a bus to Atlantic City, receive coupons for $20 in chips and receive a free lunch and a box of salt water taffy thrown in as an added bonus. Suddenly, the chance to win a teddy bear or toaster seemed less appealing.

The arrival of casinos in Atlantic City inspired me to think about other business ventures, though for several years after their arrival I continued to do well. Even until 1984, when I decided to leave for Florida on a full-time basis, a booth could

Bob with his mother and sister Donna celebrate a birthday at the house in Fords, New Jersey. (Author's Collection)

The Scirocco before it had received its personalized license plate. (Author's Collection).

make $20,000 to $30,000, a solid return at that time, even though coins comprised the bulk of the money that came through the till, which meant long hours every night after we closed working a coin machine to count all the earnings.

I was fortunate to have spent more than a decade on the boardwalk, during a golden era that would end soon after I left. It was a time when families would choose to spend their vacations and whatever other free time was available on the Jersey shore, and I was thrilled to have been given the chance to provide them with wholesome entertainment at a reasonable fee. Whether the prizes were posters, albums, shirts, mugs or even Cabbage Patch kids, something won was almost certainly more thrilling for them than that same item bought at a store.

Thankfully, the New Jersey boardwalks survived the onslaught of legalized gambling and as the increasing number of casinos began to saturate the market, families once again recognized the fun that could be had at the Jersey shore. Lucky Leo continued to work his spaces for another year following my own departure in 1985, turning the operation over to his two sons, who continue to operate the business today, the 70th year for Lucky Leo's on the boardwalk at Seaside Heights. Leo passed away on November 27, 2020, described in numerous obituaries as "larger than life" and a "beloved mentor and friend to many."

Both Leo and Bob contributed significantly to whatever success that I experienced in the years subsequent to leaving the boardwalk, but so did the numerous concessionaires I worked alongside and the people that I worked with. The lessons learned on the boards weren't ones contained in textbooks and few internships can replicate the pressure of having to innovate or die that we had to overcome on the

One of the most popular bars in Seaside Heights, JR's has been in business for more than 50 years. (Author's Collection)

FOUR: LIVING THE DREAM

Jersey shore. It was on-the-job training of the most valuable kind: one where we thrived or not based on our wits and work ethic. It was the perfect education to prepare me for what came next, but I was ready and looking forward to the challenge.

Bob with Kelli and Kristin on the carousel at Seaside Heights. (Author's Collection)

FOUR: LIVING THE DREAM

FIVE

A Whole New World

A CHANCE ENCOUNTER

In the winter of 1984, while spending time in south Florida after the end of another season on the boardwalk, I encountered a man from Michigan named Dennis Sawka and went to have a drink with him. I was working as a manager for a friend from New Jersey that offseason when I stopped into a store called The Driver's Seat that Dennis owned in the same mall where I worked. It carried high-quality automotive accessories, but these weren't traditional car parts like wrenches, oil filters and spark plugs, but car covers, bras, scale models, license plate frames, floor mats, posters, shift knobs, key chains and car care products. It was unusual to see an automotive business located in a traditional mall, because it was difficult at the time to secure such valuable retail space, so it drew me in as soon as I saw it.

The concept intrigued me, since there were numerous people in the area with a lot of disposable income and I thought that automotive accessories could sell well in both good and bad economic times, believing that during booming periods owners would want to purchase items that showed off and pampered their vehicles and in downturns would use waxes and cleaning products to maintain their older cars and keep them looking newer longer.

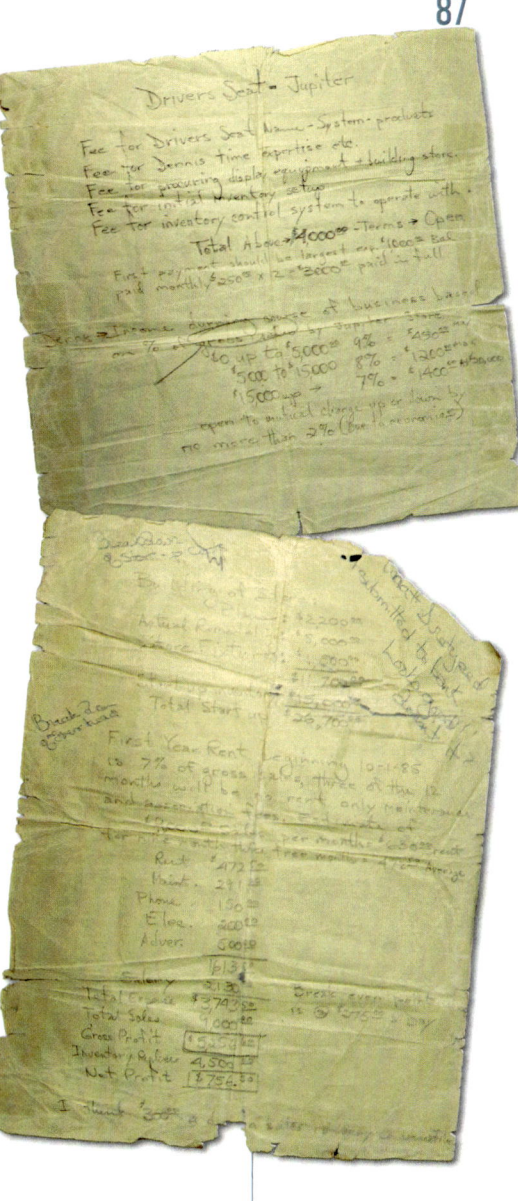

The original handwritten agreement that led to the formation of The Driver's Seat location in Jupiter, Florida. (Author's Collection)

FIVE: A WHOLE NEW WORLD

Even more attractive was the chance to run a business that operated all-year-round, rather than one that shut down in the winter months. Better yet, retail hours were much shorter than the 15 to 20 hours that I had been working on the boardwalk for the previous decade or so. One thing led to another and we decided to partner to open an additional Driver's Seat location in Jupiter, Florida.

At the time, there were two other stores, including the one Dennis had in Boca Raton, doing business under The Driver's Seat name, both with permission to use the same name from the original creators of the concept (who soon abandoned it), operating independently and carrying almost identical products, but otherwise having no tangible relationship with one another.

I returned to the boardwalk for one final year to earn as much cash as possible to start the new store in Jupiter, which would require a $4,000 payment to Dennis and an

The Driver's Seat at West Palm Beach offered a wide variety of automotive accessories. (Author's Collection)

FIVE: A WHOLE NEW WORLD

The back room at The Driver's Seat in Boynton Beach that would later house the first iteration of Palm Beach Motoring Accessories. (Author's Collection)

additional $15,000 to cover my share of operating expenses like rent, fixtures and inventory. I also planned, however, to have my girlfriend Doreen Vardalis, who later became my first wife, work at the store that Dennis operated in Boca Raton over the following summer learning the intricacies of the business from him until I could return at the end of the season on the shore.

I knew next to nothing about retail sales, but I did have all that knowledge about interacting with customers on the boardwalk and I decided to adapt those skills to work in this brave new world. As a car guy, working around things for automobiles was just icing on the cake.

When we first opened in October 1985, the area was ripe for the taking. *Miami Vice* aired on television every Friday night and the cocaine cowboys, yuppies and other conspicuous consumers weren't indisposed to pampering their luxury and exotic cars, regardless of the cost. Some owners would come in and want covers and bras to protect their expensive vehicles, others wanted clothing or sunglasses branded with the name of their favorite marque.

FIVE: A WHOLE NEW WORLD

We also did particularly well with waxes and other cleaners and a customer would look at the shelves, bewildered with all the options and ask me for recommendations. Having no experience with the product, I knew nothing and would look toward Doreen, who had spent the entire summer learning all their nuances, who would use hand signals as she stood out of the customer's sight to get me to the correct answer to find the right item to meet the customer's needs, whether it was avoiding swirl marks on black paint or removing oxidation from paint exposed for too long in the Florida sun.

I envisioned The Driver's Seat as a jewelry store for car enthusiasts, a place where the ambiance matched their expectations. Unlike a traditional outlet that sold waxes and other accessories alongside batteries and motor oil, where assistance came from a grizzled employee with oil stained fingers or a kid who had been driving for less than a year, all of our products were housed in glass display cases or placed on attractive shelves, with everything lit with spotlights to call attention to the items offered and cast them in the most flattering manner possible.

In addition to all the standard motoring accessories and car care products, we also offered custom road wheels from famous brands like BBS and bespoke steering wheels from names like Momo. Taking a cue from catalog retailers like Beverly Hills Motoring Accessories and MG Mitten, we also specialized in anything with a manufacturer's logo, even selling gold-plated emblems to replace the chrome ones that were fitted at the factories. With such a hot and humid-climate, not to mention lots of sunshine throughout the year, we sold countless sheepskin seat cover sets, which not only looked decadent, but could literally save someone's hide from burning when wearing dresses or shorts. Sheep also sacrificed their hides for replacement floor mats for Bentleys and Rolls-Royces, saving the original factory mats from wear and tear.

The customers that entered the store were a world apart from the ones that I met on the boardwalk. While we certainly had our share of wealthy individuals walk past the booths in Seaside Heights, most were modest and there with their families on vacation. In south Florida in the mid-1980s, conspicuous consumption was the norm and sometimes it seemed that the flashier the item we had for sale the better.

Inventory at The Driver's Seat in Jupiter, Florida. (Author's Collection)

KEEPING THE WHEEL ROLLING

The Driver's Seat location in Jupiter was an almost instant success, benefiting from increasing numbers of affluent residents who had moved into the area from surrounding towns. I had no idea at the time that the town's population would swell past 100,000 people, since there were fewer than 7,000 at the time, but I went with my gut instinct that the community was poised for explosive growth and was thrilled that proved to be true. The decision to extend our hours to the maximum that the mall allowed also paid dividends. We worked late on Sundays, when other stores would close for the entire day or shut their doors at 2:00 pm, since the movie theater that was located in the mall almost always generated a steady stream of customers. I used that time to write checks to suppliers, handle the payroll and calculate taxes, ensuring

FIVE: A WHOLE NEW WORLD

that every working moment was as productive as possible. We were open on Easter Sunday, Christmas Eve and every other holiday that we could get away with.

I didn't realize it at the time, but I was establishing a business model that I would follow when opening subsequent locations in the following years. That first year, I worked seven days a week from ten in the morning until nine at night with Doreen there the entire time, since spending time together at the store was better than being there alone. We planned on having children soon, which gave further incentive for us to work as hard as possible.

Following the first year, we decided to open an additional location. I had originally intended to secure a spot in a new mall in Jensen Beach, built by DeBartolo Development, who had pioneered the indoor shopping mall concept, with the principals later gaining fame as the owners of the San Francisco 49ers. I reviewed the lease, which mandated a

Custom steering wheels were always a popular item. (Author's Collection)

FIVE: A WHOLE NEW WORLD

ten-year term and required me to service all the construction costs. Doing the rough calculations, I determined that I would be overreaching at that location, instead convincing someone else to take the space.

I soon found another location at the Regency Square Mall in Stuart, where the mall operator was offering incentives such as six months of free rent and the paid for improvements, attractive terms that weren't available at the DeBartolo mall. In addition to the lower overhead that the Regency Square location promised, it was also right next to a multiplex movie theater, promising an increase in traffic like the original location in Jupiter benefited from.

THIS PAGE: The Driver's Seat in Jupiter at the Regency Square Mall. (Author's Collection

FIVE: A WHOLE NEW WORLD

What I hadn't anticipated, however, was when the DeBartolo mall opened with more features and attractions than were available at Regency Square, it siphoned almost all of the business away from the other retail shops and restaurants in town that weren't located there. It took more than six months for the bloom to fade from the rose, but that initial period at the Stuart store was arduous until traffic at the location bounced back to a sustainable level.

POWER TO THE PEOPLE

With two stores in operation, I was able to understand the business better, realizing that although both Driver's Seats locations were in a mall, we were unlike most of the other retail outlets that operated there. We were a destination store, one that people intended to visit rather than one entered on a whim. From that point forward, I trained every employee to understand that most of our visitors were there with a purpose and it was their job to identify and satisfy their wants and needs from key chains to car wax. I didn't want them to accept statements from customers that they were there to browse; no one walks into a store like Driver's Seat to browse. These were car enthusiasts and people that love cars want to spend money on them.

One of the lessons that I implemented from the boardwalk was the "step-up" pitch, giving the customer a choice to obtain something better for their money. I tried hard to offer three tiers of every item at different price points: good, better

Bob hard at work installing shelves. (Author's Collection)

FIVE: A WHOLE NEW WORLD

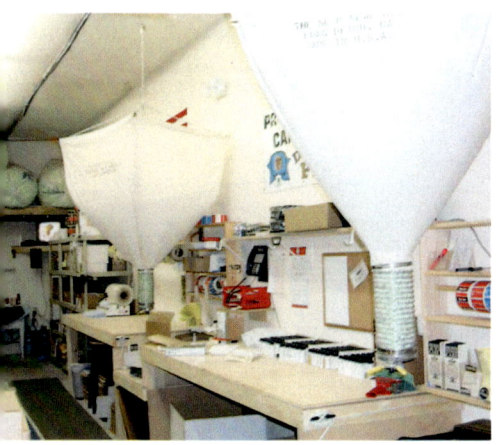

ABOVE: Bob with a new hairstyle for the 1980s. (Author's Collection)

LEFT (ALL): The showroom floor at West Palm Beach and scenes from the back room at Boynton Beach. (Author's Collection)

FIVE: A WHOLE NEW WORLD

and best. From bras, chamois, car covers and floor mats, a broader selection increased the chances to make a sale. With only 10 to 20 customers visiting each day, it was imperative to maximize the amount that each one spent.

Pricing was also important and I learned some valuable insight how customers perceived certain products. We had a beautiful display of key fobs, each with emblems of various auto manufacturers. I had an engraving machine that I had used on the boardwalk, that could inscribe someone's name on the back of the emblem, personalizing their purchase for a nominal price. These fobs were priced at $2.99, which represented a good markup from their cost of around 50 cents. For whatever reason, sales were poor and I decided to increase the price of these items to $9.95. Almost immediately,

Bob with Donna and Peggy. (Author's Collection)

FIVE: A WHOLE NEW WORLD

we sold out, proving that price is an important component of perceived quality, with too many customers believing that a key fob that cost $2.99 wasn't good enough for their BMW, Ferrari or Mercedes-Benz.

Finding the things that would make people part with their cash was harder then, because there was no internet to look up what was new and popular. Attending SEMA, the annual trade show that the Specialty Equipment Market Association sponsored, was of crucial importance in making decisions on purchasing new inventory. I would attend the show and find all the manufacturers that specialized in custom items, not the generic things you could find somewhere else, companies that sold expensive accessories like driving and fog lights, steering and road wheels, trim kits and dash covers. It was like being back on the boardwalk, hoping that whatever inventory that was purchased would resonate with customers, but unlike then, the acquisition costs with most car accessories was much more expensive than record albums and stuffed animals. That wasn't always the case, however, because we also did well in the late 1980s and early 1990s with relatively inexpensive items. At a time when car phones required an external antenna attached to the rear window, we sold thousands of fake units that gave the impression that the owner had a mobile telephone installed in the vehicle. Functional? Not at all, but the fake it until you make it mentality was alive and well even back then. In a similar fashion, when Federal regulations required that new vehicles feature a third brake light, we did brisk business in retrofitting them into older cars, making them appear as if their drivers were behind the wheel of something straight off the showroom floor.

But sometimes, we sold things unrelated to cars, like when the Furby appeared in 1998. I was able to acquire a good supply, not unlike with what happened fifteen years earlier with Cabbage Patch Kids on the boardwalk. I was stunned when I couldn't keep them in stock and was even more surprised to find people coming through the door that were looking for them specifically, rather than buying them on impulse while shopping in the store. We had people buying them two or three at a time, validating the decision to sell them.

I also learned that name brands mattered. Among enthusiasts of German cars, VDO dominated. They would purchase anything emblazoned with those three letters but avoid anything that was not. It could have been the best tire pressure gauge in the world, but without the VDO imprimatur, these customers wouldn't want them. Owners of other vehicles would want the better product,

FIVE: A WHOLE NEW WORLD

but converting those who drove Audis, BMWs, Mercedes-Benzes and Porsches was next to impossible.

The heart wants what the heart wants and successful business owners should remember to never force customers into a decision. Allow them to choose from various options, provide them the information to make an informed selection on what will best fit their needs and let them make a choice. To keep people coming back for life, give them what they want, not what you think they need.

TRAGEDY STRIKES

Doreen and I were adapting well into our new lifestyle and both stores were humming along. The location in Jupiter

Bob's parents with Doreen in Florida. (Author's Collection)

FIVE: A WHOLE NEW WORLD

had been open for around two years and the outlet in Stuart had opened and hitting stride. Everything was running as smoothly as one could hope when my world was turned upside down in an instant. I arrived to The Driver's Seat at Stuart to open for the day, vacuumed the carpet, straightened up the inventory and was greeting the first customers to arrive that morning when the phone rang.

A voice on the other end of the line asked for Robert McKee and identified himself as an officer with the New Jersey State Police. In an official tone, he informed me that there had been a single car accident on the Garden State Parkway that had resulted in the death of the two occupants, my mother and father.

Bob's parents at an American Legion event.

FIVE: A WHOLE NEW WORLD

THIS PAGE: Bob's parents at various American Legion events. The bottom pair of images were taken around the time of the Challenger space shuttle accident, which Bob and his parents witnessed from the ground. It occurred not long before his parents were killed in a single car accident in New Jersey. (Author's Collection)

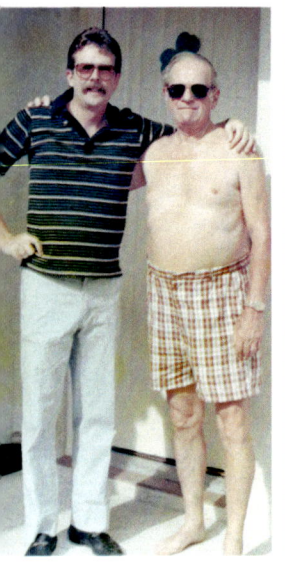

FIVE: A WHOLE NEW WORLD

The shock of the news wouldn't sink in until several weeks later, but I sat there after hanging up the handset, collected my thoughts and then hung a sign on the door that informed customers that the store would close for personal reasons until further notice. I called Doreen and both my sisters, passing on the horrible news and within a few hours was on an airplane headed to New Jersey. As such tragedies tend to do, the loss of my parents addled my thinking, so much so that I became fixated on recovering their car, a green 1987 Buick Regal coupe, from the salvage yard where it had been sent.

All the tasks attendant with the death of a family member, much less two, such as picking out the grave site, purchasing two caskets, reserving two hearses and making all the other arrangements were made in a daze. I had recently married Doreen, running two retail stores in my early 30s and having to deal with the death of both parents, my mother at 62 and father at 71, was something I had never contemplated, much less planned for.

Whatever consolation I felt came from the overwhelming outpouring of support from the boardwalk community, who offered their support in myriad ways, each gesture a meaningful beacon of light at the darkest moment I had ever lived through. While my sisters wanted to know what had caused the accident, hoping to find some reason to blame for their tragic deaths, the only thing that mattered to me was Mom and Dad were in heaven together. Until their deaths, spirituality was important, but not imperative. Afterwards, my relationship with God took on a new, more intense meaning, offering me the comfort I needed to overcome such an awesome loss.

The American Legion arranged a 21-gun salute at their service, a small tribute to a patriot that had served his country at its time of need and the woman who was his wife. Afterwards, the flag was given to me along with the shells used in the ceremony, making it an even more poignant experience. After ten days in New Jersey, I returned home, anxious to get back to work, hoping that the routine would make life feel normal again. I hadn't been in the store at Stuart for 15 minutes, when an older couple came in to purchase a sunshade for their windshield, a popular item for anyone who had spent much time in the Florida sun. After completing the sale, the man asked if I would install the item in their car if it was driven to the front of the store and given their advanced age, I agreed without hesitation.

They left to get their car and I grabbed the sunshade and met them at the front

FIVE: A WHOLE NEW WORLD

ABOVE: A portrait from Bob and Doreen's wedding. (Author's Collection)

of the store. I was flabbergasted to find that the car owned by this couple, who were around the same age as my recently departed parents, was a 1987 Buick Regal coupe with green paint and a green interior. The hair on my arms and the back of my neck stood at attention and I completed the installation without saying a word until telling them to enjoy the new sunshade right before watching them drive off into the distance.

I stood in the parking lot for several minutes, attempting to process the scene I had witnessed and finally took it as a message from God. While the death of my parents proved a horrible test of faith, perhaps the subsequent appearance of this couple was a sign telling me to trust in Him and promising that all would be fine in the future.

Both of my daughters, Kristin Lee and Kelli Ann, 'Irish Twins' born 16 months apart, arrived within two years of the accident that killed my parents and following their baptism ceremonies, I found myself becoming more active in activities at our local Lutheran church. During all the time working at the boardwalk, I had stopped attending regular church services, but the addition of two new family members, blessed replacements for two lives that had been snatched away, helped me understand the importance of putting the Lord first. Their births showed me that God does move through our lives and that He acts on his own will and timing.

FIVE: A WHOLE NEW WORLD

Doreen with Kristin and Kelli at their home in Hobe Sound, Florida. (Author's Collection)

FIVE: A WHOLE NEW WORLD

Bob with Kristin and Kelli. (Author's Collection)

While overcoming the death of both parents was an arduous process, eventually the pain of their loss was replaced with appreciation for the time I had with them. Even now, few days pass without me thinking of them and their loss, but as life returned to normal, I refocused on God and family, making plans to do more with the life I had and was fortunate to be living.

TOP LEFT: Doreen pushing Kristin on the boardwalk. (Author's Collection)

ABOVE: Kristin wearing her mother's shoes while Kelli watches. (Author's Collection)

LEFT: Kristin and Kelli with Minnie Mouse at Disney World. (Author's Collection)

FIVE: A WHOLE NEW WORLD

SIX

◊——◊——◊

Reaching for the Stars

WASH, RINSE AND REPEAT

Overcoming the simultaneous death of both parents in 1987 proved difficult to move past, but with support from family, friends and colleagues, I continued to press ahead with building upon the success of the two Driver's Seat stores in Jupiter and Stuart. Compared to my previous experience on the boardwalk, working in retail sales proved a more robust business model, mostly since turning a profit was easier with more than twice the amount of time available to generate income, not to mention having independence from the vagaries of weather.

Before long, I set my sights on not just increasing sales at the existing stores, but increasing the number of them in operation. It was imperative to understand the differences between potential new locations and I had learned a great deal from already having been in the area for two years. I wasn't

Bob in the first proper office of Palm Beach Motoring Accessories in Stuart, Florida. (Author's Collection)

SIX: REACHING FOR THE STARS

aware prior to opening the space at the Regency Square Mall, but the customer base in Stuart was conservative and hesitant to spend money and convincing customers to purchase expensive automotive accessories sometimes seemed like pulling teeth. At the store that Dennis had operated in Boca Raton, he informed me that few customers were willing to pay retail prices, making it imperative to create the perception that the existing prices reflected some real or imagined discount. To succeed, know the market and adapt to it, paying attention to demographics, economic conditions and trends or changes in what customers want or need.

Although we never altered the prices of the items at the various stores, it was important to adjust how we communicated with customers at a given location, ensuring that we tailored our messaging and sales strategies. A conservative community, residents in Stuart were hesitant to spend unless there was an obvious value proposition. In West Palm Beach, however, the owners of exotic cars seemed eager to lavish their income on them almost as soon as it was

The Driver's Seat in Boynton Beach. (Author's Collection)

THIS PAGE: The Driver's Seat in West Palm Beach (left), Wellington (middle left), Boca Raton (middle right) and Boynton Beach (bottom). (Author's Collection)

earned. It was amazing that even within the same county, different communities reflected different social and economic sensitivities. For premium products, sales staff had to radiate conviction in the benefits that the products offered, mixing in a little moxie for good measure, inspiring confidence among customers in the purchasing decisions that ultimately were made. If an owner of an expensive vehicle came into the store and balked at the $150 price for a set of personalized custom floor mats, we would ask, "how much did your car cost?" and after hearing their response suggest an alternative, like universal floor mats at a fraction of the cost, mentioning also that their neighbors and friends would admire their thrift, which usually convinced them that cheaper isn't always better.

INVESTMENT STRATEGIES

One of the recurring issues that I faced as the number of locations grew was finding managers to run them once a store had reached its first anniversary, since I continued to follow the pattern of working every available hour during that initial trial period. Often, I would look for a younger customer, one that visited a store on a regular basis, someone I knew well enough to talk with during their time browsing the aisles to gauge their communication skills and love for cars.

ABOVE: Detailing products on the store floor in Wellington. (Author's Collection)

OPPOSITE: A typical showcase at The Driver's Seat. (Author's Collection)

Sometimes, however, new employees weren't customers, but folks I met in regular life or had wandered into the store for other reasons, such as the pizza delivery kid who became an employee (later a manager and store owner) after talking to him about cars, sensing this guy was a real gearhead. I wanted automotive enthusiasts, individuals who, like me, could express their enthusiasm for our products in a manner that inspired customers to trust that we offered the best products in the world.

As the stores continued to build business, we were able to add staff, providing me the additional time to scout for new locations. This process was always done without commissioning complex market studies, little demographic research except for some anecdotal comments from trusted associates, while the stores themselves were built without blueprints or expensive architectural consultations. Moreover, assuming an executive role allowed me to spend more time with family, an increasingly important consideration in the wake of my parents' death.

SIX: REACHING FOR THE STARS

Over the next ten years, more Driver's Seat stores were opened in West Palm Beach, Boynton Beach and Wellington, Florida, joining the existing pair at Jupiter and Stuart. Each time a new store opened, Doreen and I would work there exclusively for the first year, until we could source competent staff to assume our roles, allowing us to repeat the process at the next new location.

In most instances, I would allocate a $35,000 budget to cover the expenses related to opening a new location, which would include the cost of purchasing new stock, show cases, cash registers, shelving and display stands, all pre-owned and bought from local business liquidators. I made a point to negotiate an initial ten-year lease period, with no lease payments required during the first 12 months, taking the amount of those payments and spreading them across the remaining lease payments. This meant that I only had to cover pass-through expenses in the first year, significantly reducing the amount of overhead and stress.

As had been the case with the stores in Jupiter and Stuart, I also tried to find space in recently opened shopping malls or ones under construction, making an extra effort to secure a location near a movie theater, which could provide a good source of walk-in customers to supplement regular customers and committed car enthusiasts. Amidst this period, Dennis retired and I bought his store in Boca Raton, the place that had originally inspired me to abandon the boardwalk and start working exclusively in Florida.

With strong economic conditions in the state, new car sales, especially among more expensive models, were booming and The Driver's Seat outlets became the preferred destination for owners who wanted to pamper their rides, rather than seeking out accessories at traditional auto parts stores or dealerships. When I opened the first location back in Jupiter in the mid-1980s, most of the customers that we had owned European cars from brands like Audi, Bentley, BMW, Ferrari, Lamborghini, MG, Mercedes-Benz, Porsche, Rolls-Royce and Triumph, although American models like Cadillacs, Corvettes, Lincolns and Mustangs also had their adherents.

Toward the end of the decade, however, the sports and luxury ranks swelled with the addition of Acura, Infiniti and Lexus from Japan, helping propel sales higher since these owners often had extra cash from having traded in their more expensive BMWs and Mercedes-Benzes, which saw them driving a brand new car and pocketing a substantial check for their trade-in. Often times, that cash would go towards the purchase of gold-tone emblem sets, custom seat covers and other bespoke motoring accessories for their cars, blinging them up to ensure their old ones weren't missed.

THE WINDS OF CHANGE

With six locations, each with its own manager and 20 employees spread among them, The Driver's Seat prospered throughout the 1990s. Amidst this professional success, Doreen and I were struggling. With a solid team in place at each store, the time when we would spend almost every waking hour working together was past and with two young children to raise at home, most of her time was spent with them while I continued to devote most of my attention to The Driver's Seat. Even after our eventual divorce, we would remain close, continuing to work together and I lived in the same neighborhood to spend as much time with the girls as possible.

In 1997, I turned over operational management of The Driver's Seat to Jeff Berish, who was then serving as the store manager at West Palm Beach. I wanted to devote

The Driver's Seat carried the finest car care products on the market from brands like Zymöl and Pinnacle Natural Brilliance. (Author's Collection)

SIX: REACHING FOR THE STARS

my attention to a new idea, one that I had considered for some time, the creation of a mail-order business that could allow customers around the world to enjoy the compelling motoring accessories that were available for purchase at the retail outlets. I had a friend with a successful catalog business at the time and it seemed a natural extension of the existing business.

Rather than using the established Driver's Seat brand, the new concept debuted under the name of Palm Beach Motoring Accessories (PBMA), a moniker inspired by Beverly Hills Motoring Accessories, who had first pioneered the idea of a retail store that sold automotive accessories back in 1976 and then had expanded into mail-order catalogs a decade later.

BELOW: Palm Beach Motoring catalogs. (Author's Collection)

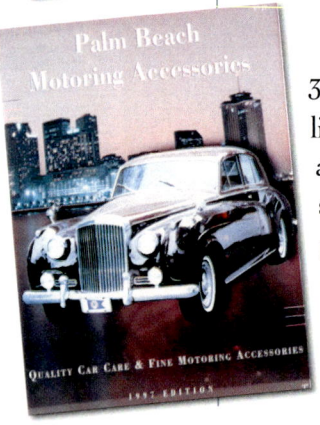

I wanted to follow the same pattern, but mixing in a bit of boardwalk selling techniques and different products from vendors that I had met over the years to make PBMA's catalog more entertaining and unique. It might seem odd to anyone reading this now in the 21st century that I started a mail-order business in the internet age, but the first commercial websites had just been active for a year when the first PBMA catalog was published and no one (especially me) could have foreseen the meteoric rise of online commerce at the time.

It took considerable investment to print 25,000 to 30,000 catalogs and send them to names on a mailing list purchased from a broker, but I took the plunge and waited for the orders to arrive. Unfortunately, sales were less than anticipated, so we went about preparing another catalog for the Christmas season. Bear in mind, that we did this is in the beginning of the summer and attempting to know what would be popular later in the year seemed like a fool's errand at times.

SIX: REACHING FOR THE STARS

Bob with his sisters in Palm City, Florida.

We purchased a new list of names, mailed out the catalogs and waited again for orders that arrived only in middling numbers. The entire operation was run out of a small 400-square foot office in the back of the store in Boynton Beach and even with that minimal overhead, the expense of purchasing the mailing lists and then printing and distributing the catalogs was exacting a horrible financial toll. Thank goodness we were able to cover the costs with the income generated from The Driver's Seat, but through PBMA's second year of existence, mail-order sales never came close to covering the operational expenses, much less able to generate a profit that could support all the time, effort and resources that were being expended.

The lone bright spot was that I had recently decided to introduce a small PBMA online store to supplement the mail-order catalog, since it had become clear that one of the

SIX: REACHING FOR THE STARS

main disadvantages that PBMA faced was stale products and pricing. With several months of lead time required to create and distribute the catalogs, it was inevitable that prices would change during the interim and what few internet retailers that existed at the time would have inevitably undercut our printed prices before the catalogs reached potential customers. PBMA's small website, primitive though it was, contributed the lion's share of revenue, not to mention required far fewer resources to monitor and update.

With four catalogs published and distributed, PBMA was at a crossroads. I had poured in all the profits from The Driver's Seat into the unprofitable operation and found myself on the brink of disaster. I was flat broke, but didn't want to admit that the entire exercise had been a disaster almost from the start. I made the decision that if PBMA was going to survive it would be as an e-commerce platform, prioritizing internet sales over the mail-order side of the business.

DESPERATE MEASURES

With no money available to put into building a more robust internet presence, much less print additional catalogs, I had to come up with a solution. Fate intervened while talking to my younger sister Peggy, while we were at a wedding at the Breakers in Palm Beach. I explained the situation and what I intended to do about it and asked whether she would loan me $25,000 to put the plan into action.

Thankfully, Peggy believed in me enough to provide the funds that would help PBMA transition from a mail-order business into an online one, betting that the World Wide Web represented the future and hoping that I hadn't made the biggest mistake ever. I was fortunate to have a young car enthusiast working across the street named Jason Sierra, who also happened to have considerable knowledge about computers and convinced him to help me bolster our internet presence, maximizing the chances that potential customers would find us near the top of their search results.

Almost all of the products available on the website were sourced from the existing inventory already in stock at the retail stores, helping PBMA weather the transition into this bold new world. It was a lean operation, with Doreen continuing to run the business and Jason handling all the technical details. I had learned at The Driver's Seat that educating customers was critical to success, providing them with information that could help them choose the best product to meet their needs helped close sales, but also created a better relationship that increased the chance for repeat business. While we couldn't speak to potential buyers online, we could educate them about the products that we offered.

At the time, most internet retailers used an image of the product, a simple description and a price in their listings, with the price often listed first. With little knowledge available at the time about how the various search engines applied their algorithms, much of what we did was trial and error, but we found almost immediate success when we started to provide extended text descriptions of our products, helping educate customers about their particular features and benefits, while listing the prices at the bottom. This kept people reading (and learning), which meant them spending more time on the website, helping push us further toward the top of the search engine rankings.

It took two years following the decision to prioritize online sales before PBMA started to record meaningful profits, but with each successive month it was becoming more

Always an avid boater, Bob at the helm of his boat at Islamorada in the Florida Keys. (Author's Collection)

evident that the choice had been the right one. Although we continued to distribute the catalogs, revenue from the mail-order business never exceeded the online turnover, which lead me to consider another momentous change, just in time for the new millennium.

A STRANGE NEW WORLD

In 2000, the web address of PBMA's online store changed from PBMA-FL.net to Autogeek.net, introducing a brand that would soon become a touchstone for customers around the world. Initially, PBMA's name had been selected to combine thoughts of Beverly Hills Motoring Accessories and images of the south Florida lifestyle that *Miami Vice, Goldfinger* and *Scarface* had helped popularize, but with the increase in the online business, a name that was both catchier and easier to remember seemed in order. I always fancied names that began with an 'A' and something with an 'auto' prefix made sense, but none of the potential candidates struck the right chord with me.

I had recently visited the Martin County State Fair in Stuart and ran across a booth there that implored visitors to 'shoot the geek,' which was the busiest attraction on the entire fairground. It featured a real person dressed as the 'geek,' who was stationed about 20 feet from the front of the booth, where a customer armed with a paint ball gun could pelt the unfortunate staffer to his or her heart's content for a modest fee. The sight of the geek wincing with exaggeration at each shot and covered in multi-colored splotches entertained the crowds to no end and stuck in my mind when it came time to devise a name.

The Autogeek name displaced the Palm Beach Motoring Accessories brand on the cover of the printed catalog. (Author's Collection)

Thinking back to the fair, I thought about the throng that surrounded the 'Shoot the Geek' booth and created the "Autogeek" portmanteau as the new name for the online store, which seemed perfectly suited for the task at hand. By the following year, the PBMA printed catalog adopted the same moniker and the transformation was complete; when the business had started, the online component was a mere supplement to the mail-order business and within five years the roles had reversed.

With the selection of available products increasing at a steady pace, thanks to the relationships cultivated with a number of vendors ever since I opened the first Driver's Seat location in Stuart, online sales continued to grow, outstripping the catalog business more than ever before. In 2002, we moved into a new 1,000-square foot unit in Stuart, providing the space needed to house the inventory and process orders for shipping to customers. The new location also allowed us to have private offices for the first time, giving Jason room to work on expanding the website's online presence and boosting the brand's new identity across the World Wide Web.

The following year we were able to add an additional employee, bringing the total to five, who photographed the stock for posting on the website and curating our online content, supplementing Jason Sierra's existing customer care team. With the business continuing to grow, I secured the adjacent unit, doubling the available space for inventory and order fulfillment and allowing for four small offices to house the administrative, creative and customer service departments.

BRAND BUILDING

The original concept for PBMA, which had evolved into Autogeek, had envisioned providing customers with the same insight into the world of high-quality automotive accessories and personal care that were available at The Driver's Seat combined with the convenience of mail-order and an almost unlimited selection of curated products. While it had taken almost five years to establish the brand as a market leader, there was little question that it was proving an attractive proposition for an increasing number of customers.

As internet sales accounted for an ever larger share of business, I made the decision in 2004 to abandon the mail-order business, printing the final catalog in 2004. By the end of the year, a dedicated crew was in place to handle order fulfillment, in addition to a bookkeeper, copywriter, marketing director, graphic artist and additional customer service representatives.

The goal of building a talented team who worked in a cooperative environment to provide the highest levels of customer service and operational efficiency had

Bob with Scoot Blank before the third Detail Fest in Stuart, Florida. (Author's Collection)

come to fruition, supporting the brand's continued growth and cementing its place at the forefront of online automotive accessory retailers. To further broaden the offerings available to our growing customer base, I continued to seek out new products that offered outstanding performance, quality and value, which had begun when an exclusive license to manufacture Pinnacle Natural Brilliance car care products was secured from Classic Motoring Accessories back in 1996 and then when we developed our own line called Detailers Pride the following year.

From the opening of the first Driver's Seat store in Jupiter and subsequent formation of PBMA and Autogeek, car care products had taken on increasing importance, attracting more customers and generating more revenue with each passing year. We had always carried the best brands available in the space, such as Meguiar's and Zymöl, aware that serious automotive enthusiasts held them in the highest regard, but as the market matured, customers wanted more choice than ever before, transforming what had once been a small niche in the automotive accessories business into a multi-million dollar segment that continued to grow at a rapid pace.

The first protective product for automotive finishes appeared in the last few years of the 19th century, not long after the arrival of the first motorcars, when animal fat was rubbed onto the exterior surfaces to protect them from the dust that was an unavoidable consequence of driving on unpaved roads.

In 1901, Frank Meguiar established a small facility in Indiana to produce furniture polish that soon began developing variants for automotive use, eventually spawning

Bob seen during his first appearance at SEMA in a space located within Eurosport Daytona's display. (Author's Collection)

the eponymous brand that remains a market leader today. Not long afterwards, George Simons developed a car care product containing carnauba wax, a concept that would later become popular with dedicated enthusiasts, though nowhere near as ubiquitous as Turtle Wax, which achieved mass market dominance following its introduction in 1944 (under the trade name Plastone) and grew into the largest car care brand in the world.

With the widespread adoption of metallic paint and clear coat finishes over the following decades, paint protection took on increasing importance with a growing legion of gearheads, creating a market that smaller companies would attempt to exploit with higher-quality products tailored for specific finishes. One of the most successful of these specialist pioneers was Zymöl, established in 1980 after

Frank Meguiar's original location in Indiana. (Meguiar's)

its inventor found a formula for wax intended for use on horse-driven carriages and had it reproduced and sold it for automotive applications. Throughout the 1980s and 1990s, the unprecedented proliferation of car care products resulted in almost too much choice for consumers.

Helping educate consumers about which product was best suited to meet their specific situational needs had been woven into the fabric of The Driver's Seat from the beginning and continued through to PBMA and Autogeek. In no small measure, we helped create the problem, offering a broader selection of car care and then detailing equipment than most automotive enthusiasts had ever seen before. We developed Cobra, a line of microfiber towels and related items, touting their merits over the old bath towels that had been used for decades. With the market making clear that it wanted products with better performance, we created new waxes, polishes and cleaners to meet the demand, each tailored to return optimal results.

These specialized products, developed with the assistance of the finest chemists and professional detailers in the business, conferred an astounding array of benefits, but required us to educate customers to help them select the right tool for the job. We soon began to research best practices, sought advice from industry leaders and then set out to spread the gospel about how to make cars shinier with less effort than anyone had ever thought possible, but that required bolstering our ranks and building the best team we had ever assembled. I hoped that we were up to the challenge.

Bob poses with a vendor at Detail Fest. (Author's Collection)

SIX: REACHING FOR THE STARS

SEVEN

Calculated Risk

REACHING OUT

Throughout the first few years of Autogeek's existence, interaction with consumers occurred much as it had before, through conversations with customer service representatives and one-way communications, first through the catalog and then evolving to content on the website and the first primitive email messages. The first software developed to support the formation of an internet forum, a place for centralized discussions to take place online, had reached critical mass during the late 1990s, but did not gain widespread popularity until the following decade, right as Autogeek was hitting its stride.

In order to take advantage of this new technology, one that would allow us to engage in conversations with customers that everyone could read and benefit from, Autogeek launched its own detailing forum in March 2006. A veritable game-changer, AutogeekOnline.net (AGO) would eventually provide us with a new channel to answer questions about our products and host meaningful discussions with a passionate group of car people who shared a common interest in keeping their vehicles looking their best.

With Autogeek's Meghan Poirier, who had been hired

Bob pictured prior to Autogeek's first appearance at SEMA. (Author's Collection)

SEVEN: CALCULATED RISK

to photograph our stock for the website, helping moderate the forum, AGO would eventually become a thriving online community in later years. Bolstering ties with our customers and all detailing enthusiasts was also the impetus for one of our most popular creations, an event that allowed them to gather in one location and celebrate their mutual passion.

The first Detail Fest was held at our facility in 2006, drawing fewer than a dozen guests, but launching what would become an industry institution that would eventually attract crowds numbering in the thousands. I ordered pizza for everyone in attendance and the afternoon was spent detailing vehicles, with Autogeek staff passing on their secrets about how to make a car shine.

Later that year, as the business continued to grow, we moved into a 5,000-square foot warehouse in Stuart, while an even bigger dedicated space was under construction down the street. Our team continued to grow as well, providing the outstanding service that customers had come to expect. It was a continuation of the stratagem I had first adopted on the boardwalk and then implemented again with The Driver's Seat. Hire the best people possible, train them well and provide them with the resources and support needed to get the job done.

OPPOSITE TOP: Bob at the second Detail Fest.

OPPOSITE BOTTOM: Bob with Chris Lamb from Grit Guard at Detail Fest. (Author's Collection)

BELOW: The Autogeek crew at SEMA. From left to right: Jason Sierra, Yancy Martinez, Pat McCall, Bob McKee, Darlene McKee, Bobby Britt, Nick Rutter and Todd Helm. (Author's Collection)

SEVEN: CALCULATED RISK

LETTING GO AND MOVING ON

As Autogeek continued to mature, running it required more and more time and energy, which until that point had been shared on an as needed basis with The Driver's Seat. Even though the retail stores remained profitable, there was a limit on the hours that each could operate. Much like had been the case with the move to abandon the boardwalk, which suffered from a short selling season, to start a business that was open the whole year long, there was no ignoring the fact that an online store never closed, allowing customers to shop on their schedule.

Although it was a difficult decision to make, I chose to allow the leases for the various retail stores to expire rather than renew them, but making an exception for two locations. In recognition for the hard work and loyalty that Jeff Berish had devoted to The Driver's Seat, not to mention his success at managing all the locations following PBMA's formation,

OPPOSITE TOP: Bob talking with two participants at Detail Fest.

OPPOSITE BOTTOM: Bob posing with two personalities from local radio station WZZR at Detail Fest. (Author's Collection)

BELOW: Bob leading the weekly all-hands meeting at Autogeek. (Author's Collection)

SEVEN: CALCULATED RISK

I offered him the chance to purchase the West Palm Beach store, which he accepted without a moment's hesitation. In a similar fashion, the Stuart outlet went to Chris Donnelly, who was the first employee hired at that location.

That both stores still continue to operate successfully is a testament to the pair's business acumen and their willingness to listen whenever I had something to contribute, which didn't happen often, but made me feel good to still offer value to the business that had given me so much. Moreover, their continued success has validated the decision to pass on the stores to them, allowing them to benefit from something that both helped build, emphasizing we're forever part of an extended family, no matter who signs the checks.

In 2008, Autogeek moved into its new 15,000- square foot building in time to host the Third Annual Detail Fest. Rather than the handful of attendees that had been there two years earlier, rabid crowds filled every available space. The still empty building housed the vendors and displays, while a popular car show was held outside, with entertainment and food provided to make it fun for the whole family.

SEVEN: CALCULATED RISK

TALENT SHOW

I have always taken pride in recognizing talent and one of the most talented individuals in the detailing business joined our team in 2009. Mike Phillips had started with Meguiar's in 2001, devoting most of his attention to teaching detailing classes to consumers, helping them make the most of the well-respected products that the company offered. He also helped develop new products, incorporating new technologies to provide better results with less effort.

As is the case with most successful businesses, Meguiar's had a great team and as accomplished as Mike was, there was someone just as talented doing the same work, which impacted his chances for advancement. Mike happened to attend Autogeek's Detail Fest in 2009 to host a detailing class with Meguiar's products. Believing that our event was merely another car show, he was impressed to discover it more akin to a smaller version of SEMA, one exclusively created for the detailing community where vendors, suppliers and customers could meet one another and discuss issues important to them. The most impactful facet of Detail Fest for Mike was the focus on teaching customers to use the available products to their best advantage, something that he considered a prerequisite for leading companies in the space.

Once we had a chance to talk, it was clear that we believed the same things and both saw the value in education as a means to building an effective brand. Although Mike wasn't aware, I watched his classroom presentation and came away impressed with his knowledge and communication skills. Afterward, we had a further talk about the event and I offered him a five-year contract and the chance to host his own detailing television show, allowing him to reach a wider audience than possible through conducting in-person events. Not wanting to undermine my existing relationship with Barry Meguiar, I asked Mike to confirm there were no issues with him joining our crew.

Unlike Meguiar's, which produced and sold its own products, Autogeek offered a wider selection for customers, selling our own house brands as well as those from other marketplace leaders, giving buyers an unprecedented choice to find the right product for their needs. With Mike on board, we rededicated our focus and energies into ramping up our education program, writing articles and books, producing videos for online distribution and holding more live events, such as the Detailing Boot Camp that was held four times a year, providing attendees three days of hands-on instruction using tool and product that Autogeek carried,

LEFT: Bob with Mike Phillips at Detail Fest. (Author's Collection)

BELOW: On the phone at Detail Fest. (Author's Collection)

arming them with the skills required to become detailing professionals or take care of their personal cars at a professional level.

With competition increasing as new players entered the market, ranging from small boutique brands to additional products available from some of the major stalwarts, I decided to sponsor a number of automotive shows on television, allowing Mike to produce small segments that appeared on them showcasing Autogeek products on programs like *Motorhead Garage*, *Two Guys Garage*, *Truck U* and *My Classic Car*.

These vignettes proved so successful in promoting the Autogeek brand that we moved on to producing two television programs beginning in 2010, both running for two seasons each. The

SEVEN: CALCULATED RISK

ABOVE: Adding an autograph to a Detail Fest giveaway.

BOTTOM: From left to right: Nick Rutter, Jason Sierra, Brian Juziak, Meghan Poirier, Mike Phillips, AJ Janic and Bobby Britt stand before an advertisement for *Competition Ready*. (Author's Collection)

first, Autogeek's *What's in the Garage?* aired on Fox Sports Network and featured Mike interviewing car owners and sharing with them detailing tips and techniques, sometimes with appearances from guest stars of the automotive world. The first season featured Mike traveling the country visiting with owners and talking with them about their cars, while the second season's episodes were filmed in our studio at Autogeek's headquarters in Stuart. Autogeek's second series was *Competition Ready*, which aired on the Velocity channel, now known as Motor Trend. Produced by the same team that brought *Overhaulin' with Chip Foose* to the airwaves, it paired Mike with Adrienne "AJ" Janic to showcase their detailing skills on some of the world's most fabulous automobiles.

SEVEN: CALCULATED RISK

Bob with AJ Janic and Mike Phillips before the first Battle of the Builders at Detail Fest. (Author's Collection)

By this time, Autogeek's stable of house brands, Pinnacle Natural Brilliance, Pinnacle Black, Wolfgang Concours Series, Detailer's Pro Series, Diamondite Glass & Plastic Care, Cobra and Blackfire covered the entire spectrum of automotive detailing and car care products, comprising some of the industry's best regarded waxes, polishes, cleaners, towels, brushes and tools, not to mention Marine 31, a dedicated line of products for boats, recreational vehicles and personal watercraft. Throughout the period, other changes helped Autogeek expand or made life easier, like switching domain names from Autogeek.net to Autogeek.com, acquiring former competitors or their assets such as Classic Motoring Accessories and Autopia. As these changes were made, PBMA became the Palm Beach Motoring Group, which served as the new holding entity for the ever growing Autogeek operation.

As social media started to supplant the forums in importance as a communications medium, Autogeek established a presence on Facebook, Instagram, Pinterest and others, always looking for new ways to connect with

Bob and Mike Phillips tossing out goodies at Detail Fest. (Author's Collection)

SEVEN: CALCULATED RISK

SEVEN: CALCULATED RISK

ABOVE: Bruno Massel, Matt Steel, Bob and Mike Phillips holding a discussion at Autogeek's Show Car Garage. (Author's Collection)

BELOW: Bruno Massel behind the wheel of his Autogeek-sponsored NHRA dragster, which he drove to a pair of Comp Eliminator titles. (Author's Collection)

customers. In addition to serving as the virtual home for Autogeek's business, the internet proved instrumental in building and expanding the brand. Almost from the beginning we advertised on Google and other search engines and soon the lion's share of our marketing budget was spent on 'pay per click' advertisements and optimizing search engine results, allowing us to reach between two and three million in sales on a good month. Although our initial returns of ten to one per dollar spent fell significantly, we continued to rely on these ads in later years and remain committed to their use now.

As effective as the internet advertising campaigns and television programs were, we also exploited more traditional marketing strategies like sponsoring Bruno Massel in the National Hot Rod Association, helping him win a pair of NHRA Comp Eliminator championships in a dragster adorned with all of Autogeek's brands! Live events also continued to provide invaluable exposure, none more important than Detail Fest, which celebrated its 10th anniversary in 2015.

Never forgetting my roots on the boardwalk, where I learned how important it was to entertain

SEVEN: CALCULATED RISK

the crowds and attract attention, I always made sure that celebrities were in attendance at our annual Detail Fests, our monthly Cars and Coffee gatherings, and other events, such as car shows, concours and trade shows like SEMA.

Among those in attendance over the years were some real stars and compelling personalities, some of whom became good friends in the process, including Dennis Gage (*My Classic Car*), Chris Jacobs (*Overhaulin'*, *Long Lost Family* and the NFL Network), AJ Janic (*Overhaulin'* and *Competition Ready*), Barry Meguiar (Meguiar's and *Car Crazy*), Matt Steel (*Truck U* and *Matt Steel Outdoors*), Cristy Lee (*All Girls Garage*), Bruno Massel (*Truck U* and *Garage Squad*), Wayne Carini (*Chasing Classic Cars*), Von Hot Rod

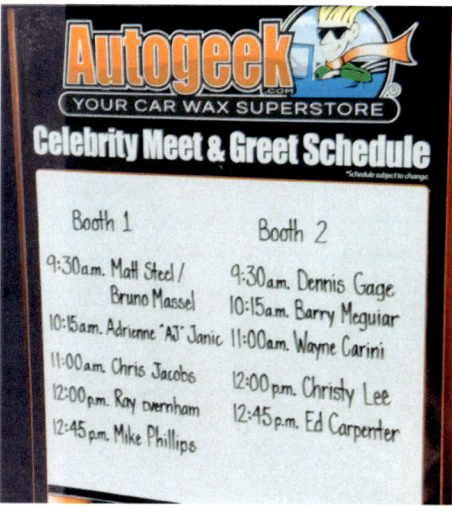

ABOVE: Automotive luminaries were a key component of every Detail Fest celebration. (Author's Collection)

LEFT: A happy group of stars at Detail Fest. From left to right: Dennis Gage, Ray Evernham, Von Hot Rod, Barry Meguiar, Mike Phillips and Cristy Lee. (Author's Collection)

SEVEN: CALCULATED RISK

(an automotive pin striper) and Ray Evernham, NASCAR Hall of Famer, former crew chief for Jeff Gordon and host of TV's *Americana*.

Their presence never failed to enhance the enjoyment of guests at the events that we hosted at the Autogeek facility or

ABOVE: Mike Phillips, Wayne Carini and Bob discuss the announcement of Autogeek's sale with Barry Meguiar on the *Car Crazy* stage. (Author's Collection)

RIGHT: An entire galaxy of stars and Battle of the Builders competitors pose for a selfie at Detail Fest. (Author's Collection)

SEVEN: CALCULATED RISK

ABOVE: Cristy Lee. (Author's Collection)

TOP LEFT: Dennis Gage and Barry Meguiar. (Author's Collection)

MIDDLE: Bob and Wayne Carini. (Author's Collection)

LEFT: Bob with Rich Evans, a custom builder from California. (Author's Collection)

SEVEN: CALCULATED RISK

at other gatherings across the country where they interacted with our customers, who loved the chance to meet their heroes up close and personal. At Detail Fest, which had become a 'must attend' automotive extravaganza for folks from almost every state, we would have not one or two celebrities, but several at the same time, allowing customers to mingle with the stars, while also getting to experience a first-rate car show, attend detailing classes and seminars and have vendors educate them about using their favorite detailing products.

SEVEN: CALCULATED RISK

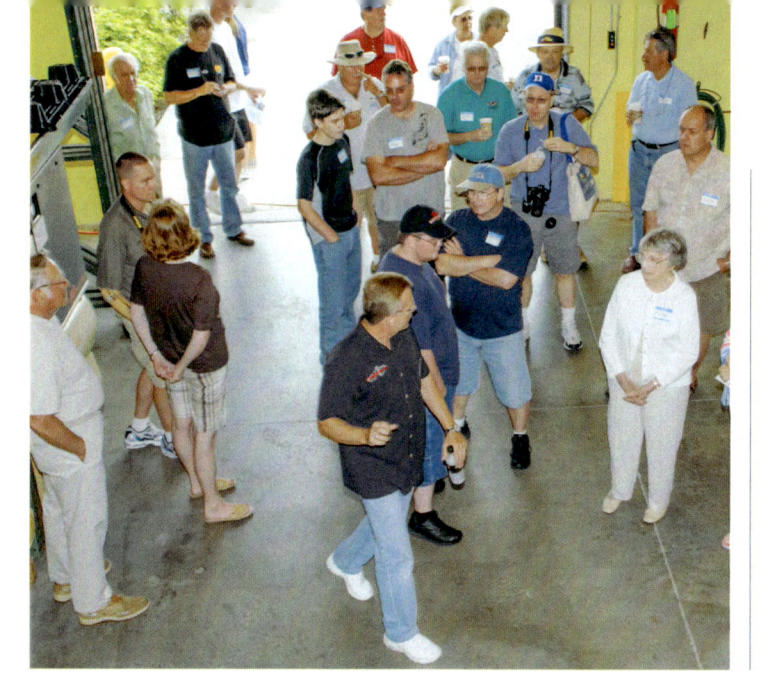

THESE TWO PAGES: In constant motion at each Detail Fest, Bob was thrilled for the chance to meet with customers, colleagues and vendors. (Author's Collection)

ABOVE: Bob discussing the merits of Detailer's Pro Series products. (Author's Collection)

TOP RIGHT: The Autogeek crew at Detail Fest. (Author's Collection)

When the last Detail Fest I was involved in was held in 2016, we had put the first event to shame, with the crowd in attendance growing from less than a dozen to more than 10,000 and two days of festivities rather than one! Even with this unprecedented success, my focus had started to wander, dreaming of new challenges and contemplating building another team to meet them. I didn't want to retire, but was open to whatever opportunities appeared on the horizon. As it turned out, I didn't have to wait long.

TOO GOOD TO REFUSE

At the same time that these thoughts were running through my head, Anton "Tony" Hulman George was looking to expand his own car care business, centered at that time around the SONAX car care brand. One of the most influential figures in the automotive industry, his grandfather had purchased the Indianapolis Motor Speedway at the end of the Second World War, allowing Tony to literally grow up in motorsports. As an adult, he raced cars, served as president and CEO of the Indianapolis Motor Speedway Corporation, founded the Indy Racing League and was co-owner of Vision Racing, one of the most successful teams in American racing.

Interested in what Autogeek could add to his existing business portfolio, Tony approached me and initiated discussions to acquire the Palm Beach Motoring Group, which included Autogeek and all its associated brands. Fearful that Autogeek had grown too big for me to devote enough time doing the things that I wanted to do, like experimenting with new ideas for products and packaging innovations, which the staff called "Bob-isms" and infusing the business with lessons learned on the boardwalk, I listened intently to Tony's proposal.

He wanted Autogeek and its brands, but not its real estate, and even better, would allow me to continue working on a new brand in our stable called 'McKee's 37,' an entry level product line under development that would mark the first time that my name appeared on products that we sold. Tony's company, Vision Investments, would take control over the Autogeek brand and its constituent parts, but rent the existing space from me under a series of one-year leases.

As far as I was concerned, the timing and size of the offer were too good to be true. It was like owning a car and

ABOVE: Taking a moment to sit and relax at SEMA. (Author's Collection)

LEFT: Bob with Kevin Byrd, Bruno Massel, Matt Steel and Brian Fuller at SEMA. (Author's Collection)

SEVEN: CALCULATED RISK

SEVEN: CALCULATED RISK

having to decide to continue working to keep it running along as always or getting a new one and making it your own. In addition to letting me retain the McKee's 37 brand, Tony would also let me handpick some old hands, individuals like Nick Rutter, an immensely talented detailer who had helped me create McKee's 37, and Joanne Young, who had assumed the same role that Doreen had held at The Driver's Seat for so long, helping me handle all the administrative and logistical tasks that every business needs to address on a daily basis.

The deal was disclosed to the public at SEMA in November 2016, with the formal announcement made on the main stage, ensuring that it was the most memorable visit to Las Vegas that I had had in almost 20 years of attending the show. With more money in the bank than anyone who had spent more than a decade working on the boards at Seaside Heights could have ever imagined, I formed Robert McKee Enterprises to house the McKee's 37 brand.

GETTING THE BAND BACK TOGETHER

Building another small team thrilled me far more than I could have anticipated, especially since Nick had become the son I had never had and Joanne never failing to do what it took to keep the new operation

Bob at the first annual gathering for McKee's 37 in Stuart. (Author's Collection)

SEVEN: CALCULATED RISK

running like a clock. I wanted to continue working with some of our celebrities, but with so much initial investment required there weren't enough funds to pay them. Imagine my surprise when Wayne Carini, who had become a dear friend, told me not to worry, he wanted to be in the Bob McKee business and accepted a small ownership stake in lieu of payment. Similarly, Nick would eventually hold an ownership stake, something I considered essential for success, since key players should have some 'skin in the game.'

Wayne Carini headlined the first annual gathering for McKee's 37. (Cape Coventry)

With the additional rental income able to supplement some proceeds from the sale, I acquired another 8,000-square foot building that would become the headquarters for McKee's 37, which we had decided to move upmarket rather than

SEVEN: CALCULATED RISK

147

TOP: Nick Rutter hosting a seminar at the McKee's 37 Trademark Garage. (Cape Coventry)

ABOVE & LEFT: The interior display area at the inaugural McKee's 37 annual gathering. (Cape Coventry)

SEVEN: CALCULATED RISK

Bob and Ray Evernham. (Author's Collection)

keeping it as an entry level brand. I charged Nick with making all of the McKee's 37 products as good or better to the other products that we had sold through Autogeek and then made the task tougher, wanting to sell them at more affordable prices, bringing high-quality car care products and tools to a broader audience. As we had done before, other brands soon appeared, Nautical One, a premier marine detailing product and Max's RV, offering the same benefits to recreational vehicle owners.

The COVID-19 pandemic boosted online sales beyond any reasonable expectation, doubling and sometimes tripling the sales volumes that we had anticipated. With the five-year term of Autogeek's lease about to expire, I decided not to renew it, allowing us to return to our original space, which seemed satisfying in myriad ways.

With Nick recently promoted to managing partner, we decided to return to our roots, creating an additional retail operation called International Detailing Supplies (now AutoForge.com) to take advantage of all the relationships, both with vendors and customers, that we had built over the years. A hybrid business with both 'brick and mortar' and online components, IDS allowed customers who had been visiting us at this same location for years to continue purchasing their favorite products in person while offering a broad selection of house brands and those from other respected and time-tested names that we had sold, but limiting them to the 'best of the best.'

At the start of 2021, renovations of our old space were complete, having installed a new roof, air conditioning units, LED lighting, an expanded showroom and a dedicated garage that could serve as both a recording studio for future television programs and classroom during live events. To mark the reopening of the building and celebrate McKee's 37 and IDS, we hosted an Open House & Detailing Expo, a new and improved version of Detail Fest, featuring several of the same attractions as before with some new elements added for extra spice. With Wayne Carini in attendance, along with other noted luminaries, an enthusiastic crowd confirmed that once again I had made the right move.

THE CHERRY ON TOP

I was having fun again, working with the best team in the world and had limitless possibilities ahead. Imagine my surprise when another opportunity came along, one that could serve as the perfect capstone to a career that had started when I was barking on the boards along the Jersey shore.

During the pandemic, a small group of old friends was working to resurrect the old SpeedVision channel, bringing back one of the most treasured names for automotive enthusiasts who loved watching automotive-themed content on their televisions for the first time when it appeared back in 1995. With Bob Scanlon, winner of nine Emmy Awards and the former president and CEO of Velocity and Motor Trend channels, at the helm of a crew that includes Business Development co-founder Tim O'Neil and former Discovery executives Joe Abruzzese and Sameel Osuri, SpeedVision is poised once again to become the definitive automotive entertainment brand on television and other media distribution channels.

Further increasing the luster of SpeedVision's return were the seed investors and content partners, individuals like Craig Jackson from Barrett-Jackson Auctions, Mike Brewer from *Wheeler Dealers*, Dave Kindig from *Bitchin' Rides*, Mark Worman from *Graveyard Carz*, professional wrestler Bill Goldberg and old friend Wayne Carini. I couldn't contain my surprise when this incredible group of individuals invited me to join them as an investor and offered me a seat on the board of directors.

With Autogeek, I had helped produce two television shows and now I had the chance to build an entire network, working alongside some of the most respected names in

Wayne Carini signing autographs for fans. (Cape Coventry)

SEVEN: CALCULATED RISK

Bob behind the wheel. (Author's Collection)

the entire entertainment and automotive industries. It almost brings me to tears thinking about my life's journey, overcoming academic troubles in school, learning how to sell on the boardwalk and then building a series of successful automotive businesses at The Driver's Seat, Palm Beach Motoring Accessories, Autogeek and McKee's 37. Whenever I decide to retire and hit the road like John Madden, traveling the highways and back roads in my luxury motorcoach, I'll know I made it from the boardwalk to the boardroom. What a ride!

SEVEN: CALCULATED RISK

Epilogue

Reflecting back on my path from boardwalk to boardroom, I'm struck with how fortunate I was to have come under the care and tutelage of so many incredible individuals starting with my parents, who never lost their confidence in me, despite all my struggles with school and the occasional teenage shenanigans that were part and parcel of growing up in the 1960s. Both sisters, Donna and Peggy, provided me with unwavering support and Peggy's loan to keep PBMA running is a debt that can't be repaid.

ABOVE: Bob's parents at a gathering for St. Patrick's Day. (Author's Collection)

LEFT: Bob and his sisters Donna and Peggy.

I always regretted making some of the same mistakes with my daughters, Kelli and Kristin, that my own father had made with me: working too hard for long hours and missing out on milestones and parts of their childhood that shouldn't be missed. It's natural that when Kristin encountered serious substance abuse problems, I blamed myself, but it's impossible

THIS PAGE: Bob and the girls. The picture from the lower right was taken prior to Kelli's graduation from the University of Central Florida. (Author's Collection)

OPPOSITE TOP: Bob and Kelli at the Omni Hotel in Carlsbad, California. (Author's Collection)

OPPOSITE BOTTOM: Kristin celebrating an arduous course marking her first year of sobriety. (Author's Collection)

EPILOGUE

to know whether things might have worked out differently had I been more involved and present in her life. Like far too many children in America, Kristin started experimenting with illicit drugs in high school, leading her down a path that few addicts survive. It was almost as if the little girl that I loved so much had been kidnapped and replaced with a different person, one that would lie, cheat and steal to get her next fix. An absolute genius, all the attributes that made her a stellar student and high achiever became a detriment once her focus turned to narcotics. Her mother and I did everything possible to provide her the help she needed to kick the habit, enrolling her in too many rehabilitation facilities in 12 years, but no amount of treatment can succeed without hard work and commitment from the addict.

It was a difficult road, involving cutting her off and refusing to answer her calls, but eventually we were fortunate and got our daughter back. She found work at a furniture store, which led her to a wonderful person named R.J. Bergstrom, who believed in her enough to hire her for an insurance position in Minnesota. She gave birth to a son, Bentley Robert McKee, dedicated herself to being the best mother possible and now runs a State Farm Insurance office in St. Paul, thrilled with the responsibilities entrusted to her and thankful to have spent almost five years sober.

EPILOGUE

Our other daughter, Kelli, struggled with the same learning disabilities that I did and her diagnosis helped me understand what I had dealt with better than ever before. I remember having to use mnemonic tricks to spell difficult words and reading and rereading textbooks to understand the material and wish that the resources that are available now had been present back then. Never having given us one ounce of trouble as a child, she has grown into a formidable adult, returning to school to get her Master's Degree in

TOP LEFT: Bob and Darlene in Carlsbad, California. (Author's Collection)

ABOVE: Darlene posed next to their original motor coach. (Author's Collection)

TOP RIGHT: Bob and Darlene at their wedding in the Florida Keys. (Author's Collection)

EPILOGUE

Clinical Psychology, having spent four years working in real estate.

Notwithstanding our divorce, Doreen and I remain close. Her contributions to the success of The Driver's Seat and Autogeek can't be ignored and that we continued to work together following our decision to go our separate ways is a testament to both her work ethic and patience.

The road to success has been blessed with wonderful times with some fantastic people. (Author's Collection)

EPILOGUE

RIGHT: Bob and Wayne Carini. (Author's Collection)

OPPOSITE TOP: Bob with Kelli and Dennis Gage. (Author's Collection)

OPPOSITE MIDDLE: Bob and Bruno Massel. (Author's Collection)

OPPOSITE BOTTOM: Bob with Mike Phillips and Barry Meguiar pose with some of the *Competition Ready* crew. (Author's Collection)

I was fortunate in later years to find another partner, one who became a treasured companion and valuable confidant. Prior to our marriage, Darlene was already a member of the Autogeek family, first meeting her when she came to visit her daughter Monique who worked in the office. Eventually, all three of her children worked with me at one time or another, along with Darlene herself, helping contribute to Autogeek's success. We were married on June 1, 2012 at an epic ceremony held at the Cheeca Lodge on Islamorada in the Florida Keys, a weekend filled with so much merriment that more than a decade later is still talked about by those who attended with fondness and awe. I've made a dedicated effort to work less in recent years and traveling in our motorcoach on various vacations and spending time together at home reinforces what I have thought all along – I have the best wife in the world.

It would have been impossible to experience the success that we had at The Driver's Seat without all the great employees that walked in the door over the years and I continue to take pride in the fact that Jeff Berish and Chris Donnelly continue to operate their retail stores successfully despite all the competition from online sellers and occasionally challenging economic conditions.

The Autogeek crew, especially Meghan Poirier, Jason Sierra, Nick Rutter, Yancy Martinez, Todd Helm, Bobby Britt, Dwayne McPeeks and Mike Phillips were all valuable contributors who helped us build something we can all look back at it with pride and membership in the Autogeek Alumni Association is a badge of honor that opened doors for several of them in later stops in their professional careers.

As for McKee's 37? When it comes time to pass the torch, I know it's in good hands with Nick, Joanne and Wayne, not to mention everyone else that helps it run like a well-oiled machine. The secret to our success has always been focusing on what customers want, something that Yancy once described as "selling happiness." From the smell and feel of the waxes, cleaners and polishes, we never lost sight of the fact that our customers were spending money on something they loved and we should share their passion or get out of the business. It's all about making them feel comfortable about spending their resources and trusting us to help them to do so.

EPILOGUE

With more friends than can be named and thanked in a book like this, two deserve special mention. When I was struggling with Kristin's addiction, Barry Meguiar shared with me his own experience caring for his daughter Nicole, who suffered from some of the same demons. His candor, caring and compassion made an incredible impression, helping me understand what Kristin was enduring and leading me to an even better relationship with Christ, a blessing that makes me forever grateful for having Barry and his wife Karen in my life.

More than a brand ambassador, Wayne Carini has been instrumental in the success of Autogeek and McKee's 37, but the support that he has always provided has been invaluable. One of the most popular and beloved automotive personalities for a reason, I'm thrilled to have him along for the ride as we bring SpeedVision back and I can't wait until our next adventure.

Whenever someone asks me to provide some advice on how to build a successful business, I have to stifle a smile, knowing that so much of what I've achieved came from nothing more complicated than simple trial and error, mixed in with some luck and good timing. When pressed, I would remind anyone interested in running an organization to build the best team possible with people who are smart, dedicated and focused on doing their best at all times. Once assembled, give them the freedom to make their own decisions, give them sound advice and guidance and never forget that everyone makes mistakes.

Although it sounds trite, trust your gut, knowing that sometimes the best decisions are subconscious, almost instinctual, ones. In a similar fashion, trust your vision, while remaining flexible enough to meet the inevitable challenges that will come across your desk.

For those involved in selling something

to someone, focus on education not price. Quality products deliver satisfaction, but a bargain rarely does. Provide your customers with the value proposition for what you're selling and let them decide what option will suit them best. An educated customer is the best customer and a satisfied one can become a strong advocate, but remember that it works both ways – an unhappy customer can do more damage than you can imagine. Don't forget the Golden Rule. Treat everyone the way you'd want to be treated and you'll never set a foot wrong. But most important, have fun!

I hope you've enjoyed this book and learned something in the process. I hope to see you on the road soon!

Ray Evernham, Chris Jacobs, Wayne Carini, Matt Steel, Bruno Massel, Dennis Gage, Cristy Lee, Barry Meguiar and Bob holding court at an Autogeek Detail Fest. (Author's Collection)

EPILOGUE

Acknoweldgements

I could never have dreamed as a child that I might get the chance to write a book, much less living a life that might interest readers. That this book exists at all is a testament to all the individuals over the years who have offered me guidance and support, none more important than Mom and Dad, who believed in whatever I did, no matter what.

My sisters, Donna and Peggy, have been wonderful siblings and I'm blessed to have them in my corner, while Kristin and Kelli, have been the best daughters a father could wish for. By almost every measure, fortune has favored me more than most, something never more obvious than when I married Darlene, who is the best partner in the world.

While Uncle Bobby and Lucky Leo Whalen had an enormous influence upon me, several others from that time working on the boardwalk also deserve special mention, among them Bob and Helen Stewart, John "The Woodman" Keane, Frankie "Pocketbooks" Sommerer, Rory Cal Maradonna, Jeff "The Cramp" Haines and Steve "Captain Beefheart" Vender.

Every employee and colleague that I have ever worked with, and alongside, deserves some credit for making all the various business ventures a success. Bob Eicheberg, Rick and Spencer Goldstein, David Stern, Butch and Sherry McCall, Renny Doyle, Terry and Jan Freiburg, Leslie and Mike Kennedy, Todd Helm and Jose A. Fernandez III from the Autogeek era were all especially valuable, while Nick Rutter and Joanne Young have been instrumental in making what has followed an auspicious encore.

In addition to their countless professional contributions, Nick, Joanne, Doreen Vardalis, Yancy Martinez and Mike Phillips all provided meaningful assistance in making this book possible; writing recollections, helping source images and all the myriad other things that needed doing on a tight deadline.

Proof that Shakespeare had it wrong sometimes, Daniel Bram provided me with stellar legal assistance from the start of The Driver's Seat through to now. Though the legal fees were enough to have paid tuition for more children than he had, Daniel's counsel was invaluable, while I cherish his friendship even more.

A special and heartfelt acknowledgement is reserved for the Hazelden Betty Ford Center in Foundation City, Minnesota, and Joe and Renee Capela. Their arduous and dedicated efforts bestowed on us a miracle, for which we will always be grateful.

Jodi Ellis worked her usual magic with the book's design and layout, literally creating something out of nothing, while the assistance that John Nikas provided in making the text more readable and entertaining proved critical in making this whole project possible. Although sometimes trying, writing this book proved cathartic, allowing me to relive the past, both good and bad. In the final calculation, the former outweighed the latter ten-fold. My cup runneth over.

As with everything, thanks to God for all the blessings that I have received, through Him all things are possible.

This labor of love has received more than its fair share of support from all quarters. Thanks again to everyone who helped along the way.

About

BOB McKEE

A serial entrepreneur, Bob McKee is one of the most successful businessmen in the automotive world. Respected for his leading role in helping create and fuel the rise of the detailing and car care market segments, he built and operated The Driver's Seat, six successful retail automotive accessories stores in south Florida, before founding Palm Beach Motoring Accessories, Autogeek.com, AutoForge and the McKee's 37 brand of car care products. A proud father of Kristin and Kelli, he lives in Stuart, Florida with his wife Darlene.

JOHN NIKAS

John Nikas is an award-winning motoring historian who specializes in compelling narratives about automotive history, while also helping write several entertaining and informative biographies in cooperation with some of the most iconic personalities in the space. John is frequently asked to speak or make special appearances around the world, discussing a wide range of automotive topics. Known for his authoritative knowledge, quick wit and entertaining delivery, he also serves as the Co-Executive Director of the Madison Avenue Sports Car Driving and Chowder Society and Automotive Engagement Ambassador for Hemmings.